EMOTIONAL EDUCATION

The **A.R.T.** of Teaching Children

EILEEN JOHNSON

A Primer For Teachers
And Parents

AVELINE
B O O K S
New York

AVELINE
B O O K S

Copyright 2017
Eileen Johnson
19 Stuyvesant Oval
New York, NY 10009

Graphic Design: Scott Johnson

Cover Illustration: Avedis Minasian - "It's me!"

THIS BOOK IS DEDICATED
TO
GERALD F. SCHOENEWOLF
MENTOR AND INSPIRATION

THANK YOU TO ALL THE TEACHERS WHO HAVE THE
COURAGE TO TRUST THEIR INNER GUIDE TO
INSPIRE THEM TO ACTION OR TO SILENCE.

IN MOMENTS OF CONFUSION AND CONFLICT, MAY WE
HAVE THE PATIENCE TO WAIT FOR OUR CREATIVITY.

AND MAY WE HAVE THE UNFAILING FAITH
IN CHILDREN THAT THEY HAVE IN US.

CONTENTS

INTRODUCTION
WHAT IS EMOTIONAL EDUCATION?

A four year-old boy and I are in a schoolyard:

> ***EILEEN:*** *Wallace, it's time to go inside now, we're done playing in the yard, come on, let's go, we need to wash our hands and then get ready for snack and circle time. (Wallace ignores me and keeps playing.) Wallace, I don't want to ask you again.*

> ***WALLACE:*** *No! I'm not going. (Wallace's cheeks are bright red. He's been playing a lot, climbing and running, and is flushed with excitement and energy).*

> ***EILEEN:*** *Yes. It's time to go in.*

> ***WALLACE:*** *No! I'm not going in. (The flush is deeper now, fed by anger, and his eyebrows are lowered, his hands on his hips. He stands his ground, he means business).*

> ***EILEEN:*** *Wallace, that's it, I said we're going in, I'm not going to say it again. Go inside now. (I have one hand on my hip, the other one pointing to the door, and the tone of my voice and expression is meant to convey that I mean business too).*

WALLACE: *(Stomping towards the door) I hate you, Eileen!*

EILEEN: *I hate you too, Wallace! Matter of fact I think I'd like to throw you out the window.*

WALLACE: *Well, if you do that then I'll come back in and I'll chop your hands off.*

EILEEN: *Really? Well, if you do that I'll shoot fire out of my eyes and you'll be all burnt up.*

WALLACE: *Well, if you do that I'll freeze you with my freezer power that shoots right out of my hands and you can't move. (Wallace and I have been moving forward as this exchange carries on, and we are now inside at the sink. Wallace is animated and engaged with me while he washes his hands. He's clearly dreaming up further schemes to annihilate me.)*

EILEEN: *Well, if you do that then I'll unfreeze myself and send you in a rocket ship to the moon.*

WALLACE: *Well, if you do that then I'll come back down and I'll cover you with a rock and no one will see you again. (Now we are in the classroom).*

EILEEN: *Oh no! You beat me! I can never win against you! Hey Wallace, would you like a snack, come over here I have some nice crackers, sit at the table. We can play this game again later. (Wallace is eager to keep up the game but at this point I know he needs to calm down and transition into snack time, so we can have the whole group move on to the playful learning activities we have planned for them. He has calmed and starts eating and chatting with his neighbors.) He is happy he defeated me in our epic 'battle.' He doesn't realize I have won too, since he is now sitting at the table doing what I had wanted him to do. Actually we have both won. We've been authentic with each other and there is no residual anger because of it.*

This story is a good illustration of how Emotional Education works. Wallace and I had played this kind of game before so we both knew how it went, and though he had never flat out said he hated me before, I knew he was capable of fiery anger, as many children are at this age.

Since we had been playfully open with each other before, he and I both understood the ground rules – it is a game of words where only imaginary weapons are exposed. In a situation of tension I was able to be real with him by playing this game. I did it in order to be authentic with him about my feelings and to give him permission him to be authentic with his feelings. I did not act shocked or censor his words, I accepted that, for one moment, he hated me because I was preventing him from having fun. What happened between us was a healthy, imaginative, non-threatening way for both of us to express our negative feelings in the moment. He was annoyed, and so was I, and rather than covering it up I decided to take the lid off and let it show.

When Wallace says: 'I hate you,' what he means is 'I am angry.' Children experience anger because they know they are small, and they feel helpless. Many parents and teachers would be tempted to say: 'Don't say hate, it's a bad word!' They might want to suppress the word 'hate' because they have associated it with other, more adult meanings that word has accrued. Adults often confuse a child's words and think it is a permanent judgment rather than an expression of temporary rage and frustration. When a child says 'I hate you!' it's not the same as an adult saying 'I hate all Irish people,' a prejudice that accumulates over time. Children are not capable of making these kinds of judgments, their emotions are transitory and their values only become entrenched after years of reinforcement by adults and their own experience.

Some adults might not like the idea of being 'hated' by their child, or challenged as an authority figure. They might not like the idea of having anger directed at them. By suppressing the WORD they might think they are controlling the feeling. Of course it is much better to accept a child's feeling and work with that. Once you shut down the expression of anger, you have no way of understanding where it came from, what it means, or how to help the child to understand it himself, and ultimately communicate and control it. If a child says 'I hate you,' it's best to ask calmly why.

In the case of my interaction with this child, reprimanding Wallace, or telling him to be quiet would have been unproductive. By letting him say what he wanted, and by countering with 'I hate you too,' in effect I allowed him to have his feelings, and I also put us both on the same hierarchical level, thus eliminating the power struggle. Sometimes it is hard for parents to let go of engaging with a child in a power struggle. They think they are going to lose the child's respect if they don't act as if they are in charge of every situation. In this case I felt emotionally strong enough to know that I didn't have to play the 'authority figure,' and I knew I could just engage with the child on a feelings level, a playful level. I could trust myself, and him, enough to know that we could grapple with negative emotions and work through them. This was done by playing a game, which is an effective way for children to learn.

Some people think that expressing anger in words can lead to an escalation, but the opposite is true – a healthy expression of anger can be a real relief to everyone. There is nothing more frightening to a child than to know that an adult is harboring anger but not showing it. Being open about your anger (in a non-threatening way) is a relief to a child, who senses that it is there, even if you don't say it is. You can say: 'I feel angry because I feel you are not listening,' which is not the same as saying: 'You're not listening!' Or you can pretend you are not angry. Hidden anger can be very scary, even if the words don't appear angry, a child can tell an adult's real feelings and intent. For instance an adult can say to a child: "No, sweetie, I don't think so," in a tone of voice that makes a child feel intimidated, and unsure of himself, because it is masking anger, and you can be very sure that children understand the hidden emotion.

However, healthy communication depends on HOW anger is expressed, and that will be discussed further in this book. Children – and a lot of adults – need to learn how best to share our feelings. It is not OK for an adult to vent feelings on children, to blame them for their own anger, or to make a habit of sharing their problems with them. Venting means letting anger out at the world without ownership of the feeling. There is a skill to accepting responsibility for how we feel and expressing it as OUR feeling and OUR perception of the world. There is a way of sharing anger that is acceptable, and many of us do not learn it, so we get ourselves into situations where bad feelings just escalate, rather than dissipate. That's why we all need Emotional Education!

This particular example with Wallace shows how an emotionally safe classroom can operate. In this case, Wallace and his teacher have a real exchange of feelings in a fun way, which allows aggression to be expressed. Because it's fantasy and because it is expressed openly, it is non-threatening. Both of us can express our anger impulses, our irritation at one another and our frustration at the conflict between us (me, wanting him to follow my agenda, and he wanting to have his own way and follow his own agenda). And it is done through a game.

The child fully understands that it is fantasy. If he believed that I really was threatening him, he would have looked scared and shut down, he certainly would not have participated in the exchange. And if I thought he was too sensitive to handle this play aggression, I would not have started it. But he and I have a strong relationship built on trust over the time we have been in class together, so when I say I want to throw him out the window I already know that he is not afraid of it actually happening.

Wallace participates because he knows it is a game. He likes that I am saying what I feel instead of pretending to not have any feelings about his resistance. He counters with his own aggression, and the exchange becomes enjoyable to both parties, and of course, I always let him win in the end. It's not a game where I am trying to defeat him, it's a game where I am letting him show his feelings, and giving him the victory. It should always end with the adult saying something like: "Oh dear, you always win!" That makes a child feel powerful, which every child wants – after all, children are acutely aware of how small and powerless they are.

NOTE: This kind of game is not for everyone. Some children are very sensitive, they do not have the courage to express negative feelings openly, or to hear negative feelings expressed by others, and would be scared by this exchange. Some children do not feel able to tell the teacher they hate them, like Wallace can. It takes a lot of self-confidence and trust for a child to say this to an adult or authority figure, and rather than being horrified, adults should be glad the child is expressing his anger openly. Parents may need to be careful when they play this game, making sure that a child is not afraid of the parent's anger.

If you do play this game you must remember it is NOT a competition, you are an adult and at the end you must present yourself as the loser: "Oh no, you beat me again! GRRR why can't I win? You're so powerful!" is a great response every time the child comes up with a good way to crush you. They love this. Wallace does not necessarily need victory, he is very resilient and just enjoys the combat, whether he 'wins' or not.

Footnote to the story:

Next day Wallace throws himself at me for a hug and I say to Wallace: "Hey Wallace, yesterday we hated each other and today we love each other – love, hate, love hate, isn't that funny?" Wallace laughs and repeats the phrase: "love, hate, love, hate..hahaha, yeah, funny." He understands, better than many adults, that hate is just a word that means angry and he knows that you can love someone and be angry at them all at the same time, and he also knows on a visceral level that being able to express negative feelings with someone brings you closer together with that person.

The word 'hate'

It is fine for children to say the word 'hate.' They should be able to say they hate disgusting smells, certain tastes which repel them, loud sounds, and so on. These gut feelings are a child's intuition, warning signs about what is not helpful or authentic. It is vital for a child to develop intuition about other people and about situations which may be dangerous. For instance, a child might say: 'I hate bananas that are brown and mushy!' and that's a good thing, they can instinctively tell that this is a sign of decaying fruit, and they should not eat it. They might say 'I hate when Mr. Brown hugs me,' and this may be an instinctive reaction to something they feel is not comfortable – also an intuitive self-protective feeling. However, in a social situation we need children to learn that repeatedly saying they hate their friend/parent is not helpful to either side because it does not bring any insight, we want to guide the child towards expressing the real feeling and understanding why they feel it.

As time goes by, we work on having Wallace say to me, and to his friends when a problem comes up between them: "I am angry at you," since it is more productive than saying 'I hate you.' This way he can begin to reflect on the fact that he feels angry. The next step in the emotional education of Wallace is for us to bring him to the point where he can say in words why he feels angry: "I am angry at you, Eileen, because I want to keep playing," or "you are telling me to go inside and that makes me feel very frustrated."

Being able to gain an insight on what he feels, and naming that feeling, gives the child the key, which releases him or her from the imprisonment of tempestuous feelings. The response we would have to Wallace saying he is frustrated would be: "I see. You are feeling very frustrated." We would not try to rush forward into getting him to do what we want, but we would let him sit with his own feeling for a few minutes. Accepting his own feelings and taking responsibility for the fact that this is HIS feeling and no one else's will help him work towards complying with the directions he doesn't like. He needs time to process his feelings before he 'gets over' them. Once we let him know we see and accept his turbulent feelings, he will come to his own way of resolving his difficulties.

When Wallace is working with another child we will encourage the other child to respond. So if Wallace says: "I'm angry at you!" to another child, we would say: "How does that make you feel, Lucy? And Lucy might say something like: "Well I'm angry at you for being angry at me." It is important for each person to express what they are feeling. Once expressed, feelings tend to evaporate. The children in this situation might even laugh at the idea that one person is angry and the other person is angry at them for being angry, they can see the humor in that. In any case, once both children express their feelings, they will develop better understanding of each other. The important thing for adults to remember is not to squash the initial expression of feelings in a child – even if they are shocking or repellant to us. We must accept that they are valid for that child in that moment.

This story illustrates the point that in a school of Emotional Education, a child can feel safe to tell the teacher anything, even that he feels intense anger towards her, and the teacher can hear those feelings without judgment, and be authentic with her feelings too. That is the goal.

Emotional Education means a number of things, and is built on the A.R.T. (Accept/Reflect/Teach) principles, which will be outlined below. Children are allowed to have their feelings, and are trained in how to express those feelings in safe and appropriate ways, which build strong relationships and healthy communities. This book will explain those principles and some of the methods of Emotional Education.

Stay tuned, our book will finish with another story about Wallace. We will see how much he grows over the course of his three years with us, and how his emotional openness and his willingness to express his feelings gives him a skill that many adults lack, an emotional awareness that will help him in all aspects of his life.

EMOTIONAL EDUCATION

Chapter 1
WHAT ARE EMOTIONS?

How many of us really know what we are feeling from one minute to the next? How many feelings do we have in a day? How many emotions are there? Can you define your subtlest feelings? It is amazing to think that we know so little about our own emotions, even though they are probably the most important motivating factor across our entire lives, shaping our destinies like hidden currents under the surface. Philosophers have been pondering about emotions for thousands of years, just like astronomers of old pondered about the stars. According to the Stanford Encyclopedia of Philosophy:

> *No aspect of our mental life is more important to the quality and meaning of our existence than emotions. They are what make life worth living, or sometimes ending. So it is not surprising that most of the great classical philosophers – Plato, Aristotle, Spinoza, Descartes, Hobbes, Hume – had recognizable theories of emotion, conceived as responses to certain sorts of events of concern to a subject, triggering bodily changes and typically motivating characteristic behavior.*[1]

Emotions are in fact, the predominant subject of most of the great philosophers. How our emotions (or Passions as they were often called) differ from 'Reason' or 'Intellect,' was the major theme. The key issue with which they struggled was in essence how emotions can be defeated or tamed. Some philosophers thought that there are two

1

forces, Reason and Emotion, and these were constantly at war against each other within us. Very often they proposed the idea that Reason was the most important force, and that Emotion should be subservient to Reason. They often observed the damage that emotion could wreak in a family, or in a nation, and they feared its destructive power.

David Hume, the 18th century Scottish philosopher, argued that we are fundamentally emotional beings. He maintained that all our decisions, and even our ideas come about from our emotional reaction to the world, and that in fact there is no objective reality without emotional response. He was very much ahead of his time when he stated that:

> *Reason is, and ought only to be the slave of the passions, and can never pretend to any other office than to serve and obey them.*[2]

He also had an insight into emotions that we are only now aware of – the fact that they are constantly changing and ever present, even when we think we are being rational:

> *The second property, which I shall observe in the human mind, is a like association of impressions or emotions. All resembling impressions are connected together; and no sooner one arises, than the rest naturally follow. Grief and disappointment give rise to anger, anger to envy, envy to malice, and malice to grief again. In like manner, our temper, when elevated with joy, naturally throws itself into love, generosity, courage, pride, and other resembling affections.*[3]

However, it was not until the early 20th Century when Freud and others began their work in this area, that there was a general recognition that emotions had a tremendous effect on our behavior, whether we knew it or not. These students of human motivation realized that emotional suppression caused illness. This new realization came about through studies of people who had symptoms of illness that were puzzling to doctors, because there was no underlying illness there. Closer study revealed that a person's emotions can be so powerful as to induce bodily symptoms – even paralysis.

A number of these philosophers/medical doctors began to think that there was a large part of us that was unconscious, a deep well of emotions that lay beneath the surface, controlling our reactions to everyday situations, that was called the unconscious. This well of emotions was of necessity kept out of sight so we could function on a daily basis. Some emotions were felt by their clients to be dangerous, because they were too painful and would destroy the person's well being, so they could not be even allowed into consciousness. (Think of people with PTSD who have to suppress upsetting memories.) Yet these emotions made themselves known on the surface. in the form of physical symptoms, phobias, and unpredictable behaviors, which were often destructive to the individual's life and success.

From this early 20th century beginning there arose a science of emotions that had a goal of analyzing the structure and origin of emotions, and their effects on our behavior. The emotional life of the child, and the mechanisms through which we gain mastery of ourselves, became the topic for the great new subject of the twentieth century – psychology.

This field has evolved rapidly, and there is still a great deal of study to be done on the emotions. Even though they are the most powerful motivating factor in our lives, we still do not understand them in all their complexity. However, all psychologists agree that the early years of childhood are when emotional regulation is learned. A child learns whether or not feelings are accepted, and to what extent. And he or she learns a method of managing feelings of all kinds, depending on the feedback of those most important in the family.

Recent educators and philosophers are growing more aware of the positive power of the emotions – as a fire that fuels our actions, a fire that can be harnessed, contained, and utilized. We do not look on Reason as the enemy of Passion. One is not superior to the other. As Freud pointed out, our Id (deep instinctive feelings) and our Superego (reason, conscience) must work together, and be controlled by our Ego (healthy self-esteem). There should not be a split between what we feel and what we know is right. Our emotions are a necessary part of us, and they should be integrated, not segregated. It is a question of self-acceptance.

If a person is too controlled by his Id, he will not be able to stop himself from acting out, being aggressive, selfish, impulsive. If a person is too controlled by her Superego, she will not be able to tolerate any faults or weaknesses in herself. Being able to laugh at oneself, or accept that we can make a mistake or fall short of other people's expectations, or tolerate one's own angry and uncomfortable feelings, is the mark of a healthy Ego.

More and more psychologists are realizing the importance of having children understand their emotions from a very early stage. They realize that we should not just be teaching children about academic subjects, we should be teaching them about their inner lives, because you cannot separate the two. Success in life means not just being able to focus on abstract problems, it means being able to work well with others. The practice of mindfulness means being in the moment and being aware of what is going on inside us. When we regularly practice reflection when we stop and look inside, we become more and more in tune with our emotions.

Being in tune with our own emotions makes us more in tune with the emotions of others. And knowing how others feel is a vital life skill. A recent book: "Unselfie," explores the idea that the very key to our survival as a society is being other-directed. Empathy, understanding, emotional connection, the author maintains, are what make life truly satisfying. But more than that, empathy can improve the mental life of individuals and the well-being of our interpersonal relationships, as well as improving society as a whole. The author, Dr. Borba, refers to a series of studies on children's pro-social behavior and says:

> Science confirms that babies are born to be social and are hard wired to care, but there is no guarantee. The habit and skill of emotional literacy must be nurtured. Teaching children an emotional vocabulary, talking about emotions, sharing their feelings, and tuning in to others, are vital for raising empathetic UnSelfies....The Empathy Advantage of teaching this habit is huge: kids who are adept at recognizing, understanding, and expressing their emotions are healthier, more resilient, and more popular; they do better in school; and they are more apt to help others.[4]

Dr. Henri Parens, Holocaust survivor and author of many publications, has done a great deal of research into childhood emotions, primarily aggression. He has studied the way this natural impulse, so important for survival, can evolve in a healthy way or turn into extreme forms of violence and sadism. His work with children leads him to the conclusion that emotional education in childhood can have a huge impact on society. In his book Aggression in Our Children, he states:

4

Our aggression – in its forms both of assertiveness (nondestructive aggression) and of hostility and hate (hostile destructiveness) – influences our emotional development, the formation of our personality, the state of our emotional well-being, and our mental health. We cannot emphasize too strongly that helping our children learn to handle their aggression constructively has large implications for their well-being and development as individuals and social beings.[5]

Given his experiences during the Holocaust, it is not surprising that he realizes the importance of dealing with aggression in society. Accepting aggression as a normal impulse and helping a child channel it into creative expression and useful pursuits is one of the most important aspects of Emotional Education.

EMOTIONAL EDUCATION

Chapter 2

THE NEED FOR EMOTIONAL EDUCATION

SOCIETY AND EMOTION

Our world is full of anger, hatred and aggression. Our world is full of sadness, despair and depression. More people are on anti-depressants than ever before. More people are obese. More people are killed in violent incidents. More people are taking drugs and abusing alcohol. And there are more suicides, because people just cannot find the happiness they desire in a world that seems alien and cold to them.

What can we do about it? What one thing would help people to be at peace with themselves, with other people and with the world? First let's ask what it is that makes people unhappy. It's not their intellect, not their body. It's their emotions. Things go wrong in life for everyone, no matter who you are. However, you can be happy or sad, depending on how you handle those things that go wrong. Some people experience tremendous stress, go through serious challenges, face incredible opposition, and yet they persevere and succeed. Other people come up against small obstacles, receive unfavorable reviews, and they give up. They fail at one thing and they think they are failures, they see themselves as helpless and small, they are angry at the world, and they feel defeated.

Why do people react in such different ways to challenges? The secret of being happy and successful is how we handle our emotions. It is not the obstacles that we come across, it's the way we handle those obstacles that matters. To be masters of our own destiny, we need to understand and manage our own emotions.

But how do we learn to be in control of our emotions? We learn in childhood. In the old days there was no sex education, children just picked up hints and clues from other people. Emotions have often been handled like that in families. Very often you have an emotion, but you are not told what is going on inside you so you feel confused and alone. For instance, not many parents explain to a child what anger is, or give ideas on how the child should handle it. Instead they see the expression of anger, fear it, and tell the child to stop. Some people think emotions should not even be talked about, they are taboo, much like sex.

Many people have to figure their emotions out all by themselves, and find their own way of expressing feelings in a healthy way. They copy other people, or maybe they are lucky enough to have a parent or benevolent adult who guides them along the way and teaches them what emotions are, where they come from, and how to manage them. But we shouldn't have to hope to be lucky in figuring out our feelings. We should be taught about our feelings as a matter of course.

There is a healthy way to show feelings, and if we can learn to share feelings with others, we can build healthy relationships and a healthy society. Feelings should not be dirty secrets that we have to keep to ourselves. A lot of bad things happen when we cover up feelings. And a lot of bad things happen when we act out our feelings in inappropriate ways. We don't have to look too far to see examples of both of these unhealthy patterns.

Adolf Hitler was viciously beaten by his father when he was a little boy. Adolf tried to do everything perfectly in order to avoid these terrible tirades, but nothing prevented his father from acting out his feelings on his child. The child was a helpless victim of his father's rage, and helplessness is a terrible feeling, it leads to feelings of isolation and deep rage.

Adolf bottled up his feelings. The child did not want to feel vulnerable to his father's punishments, and so he learned to show no pain when he was beaten. He refused to cry. He came up with a game of counting in his head the number of lashes his father gave him, and the counting gave him some sense of control. It kept him from crying so he could repress the feelings of pain and anger. Keeping his feelings inside helped him survive the beatings.

I think we all know how that survival technique worked out. Not very well for him, or for the millions of people on whom he subsequently vented his feelings of helplessness and rage. Feelings kept inside are toxic and will have an effect sooner or later. They can be acted out on others – co-workers, children, spouses, even a whole nation. If they are not acted out on others, they may take a toll on the self, in the form of panic attacks, ulcers, high blood pressure, heart attacks, alcoholism, depression, and even suicide.

So keeping feelings inside, or releasing them in destructive ways is deleterious to the self and to society. We need to learn how to share our innermost feelings with others in a safe and healthy way that promotes understanding of ourselves and others. And the most important feelings to share may be the negative ones, since they are the ones that gnaw at us inside.

The tiny country of Bhutan literally measures its country's GNH – Gross National Happiness. Their focus is the well-being of their citizens, it is the most important measure of success in this land. Compare this with other countries, which measure Gross National Product. At a workshop in 2009, experts from around the world convened to design an educational system that would reflect the values of Bhutan and encourage the development of the human being and society.

> Several proponents, including the country's Education Minister himself, have emphasized that genuine GNH curricula would go beyond mere conceptual and intellectual learning but attempt more effectively to integrate heart, mind, spirit, and behavior (or action). In other words, such curricula would incorporate learning that draws not only on reasoning alone but also on experiential, artistic and feeling faculties, and that attempts to translate knowledge into action. For example, some Bhutanese educators and policy makers suggested that GNH curricula might also include community service and voluntary action that nurtures compassion and care for others.[6]

9

The Bhutan education system is designed to incorporate daily reflection and meditation as well as care for the environment and work in the service of the community. This country, sandwiched between India and China, has one of the best environmental ratings in the world, and is proud of its dedication to the value of human fulfillment over any other. If a tiny country can do this, why can't we?

SCHOOL AND EMOTION

There is a growing awareness of the correlation between emotional intelligence and academic achievement. Daniel Goleman's book "Emotional Intelligence" when it was first published in 1996, drew attention to the importance of emotions in our school and work lives. It is now in its 10th edition, with worldwide sales over 5,000,000. It has had a profound influence in the intervening years, with many more schools now paying attention to the need for focusing on the emotional life of the child. The book points to the connection between emotions and academic achievement:

> ...emotional literacy programs improve children's **academic** achievement scores and school performance. This is not an isolated finding; it recurs again and again in such studies. In a time when too many children lack the capacity to handle their upsets, to listen or focus, to rein in impulse, to feel responsible for their work or care about learning, anything that will buttress these skills will help in their education. In this sense, emotional literacy enhances schools' ability to teach.[7]

More and more studies are proving what we all know instinctively – that a well-adjusted child will learn more easily and retain more than a child who is stressed, impulsive, depressed, or otherwise bogged down with emotional issues.

A working paper by Gabrieli, et al, outlines the current research on the correlation between 'non-cognitive skills' – that is emotional intelligence – with school performance. There are many studies discussed in this paper, and they all bear out the importance of what they call non-cognitive skills in education. They note that:

> A meta-analysis of 213 social and emotional learning (SEL) programs by Joseph Durlak and his colleagues also found strong social-emotional skills predicted positive academic outcomes.

The goals of social-emotional learning programs included developing self-awareness, self-management, social awareness, relationship skills, and responsible decision-making. The authors found students who participated in the programs developed greater social-emotional skills compared to their peers in the control groups. In addition, they found improved academic outcomes, measured by both standardized tests and school grades. Students participating in SEL programs had an 11-percentile-point gain in achievement, as compared with the control groups. These program effects also showed that these skills can be strengthened through specific interventions, demonstrating the underlying malleability of non-cognitive skills.[8]

In other words, we can work on emotional skills such as self-control, self-awareness, and social awareness, and make lasting changes in how a child copes with obstacles and frustrations. The same paper mentions that these skills can be developed at an early age, thus putting children at a great advantage for the rest of their lives. This is particularly relevant for underprivileged or high-risk populations. The development of emotional regulation can make a huge difference for children struggling with family and economic stressors:

This study also compared the effects of the (emotional skill development) program on students in high-poverty schools and students in either low-or medium-poverty schools. Some of the gains were consistent across all levels of income, while other gains, such as those in vocabulary, were specific to students in high-poverty schools. According to the researchers, these findings suggest "a focus on executive functions and associated aspects of self-regulation in early elementary education holds promise for closing the achievement gap." (page 13)

Many children feel disconnected from school. There is a large dropout problem in the Unites States. These dropouts include children who do not fit into the mold, due to different abilities, and they also include children for whom school seems irrelevant, or even oppressive. This dropout problem is serious because those who drop out are often at a huge disadvantage in an already overcrowded job market.

Some schools seem to think of children as machines, walking brains without a body, without feelings. That is a shame, since many children come to school feeling worried, ashamed, nervous, shy, angry, lonely, insecure, pressured and so on. These feelings interfere with cognitive functioning and performance in school. If there were a period each day when children could connect emotionally with an empathic adult and find the words to express their inner world, then this would free them up greatly and allow them to connect with their schoolwork and cooperate with their fellow students. If children could realize that they are not alone, others feel sad, lonely, scared, and so on, they would build meaningful supportive friendships. Bullying would not get a chance to take root, because bullying begins in insecurity and loneliness and thrives in an atmosphere where people don't share feelings and suffer in silence.

A school where children's emotions are actively engaged is more involving and inclusive, and children feel motivated to learn when they can be open and listened to. The emotionally responsive curriculum would have as its goal the creation of a healthy community in which everyone can feel safe and trusting. Children would rush to school, much like they do in our school, where we create a safe, open, welcoming environment and children can be themselves.

Teachers teach better when they understand a child's feelings

Understanding the child's emotional life is an essential task for the educator, for a number of reasons. One of those reasons is that real learning, the kind of learning a child remembers, is done through emotional engagement in the work. Many studies have been done on the process of recall, and all these studies demonstrate what we all know instinctively – that people recall vividly, and for long periods of time, events which have a high emotional impact. Ask yourself where you were when you heard a piece of shocking news – chances are you remember every detail of the place and time Other days slide by without being retained, because there is no emotional component. You probably remember 9/11/01 vividly, but you've forgotten all about 5/11/01 – unless, of course it was your birthday or you won the lottery, or a loved one died. Memory is intricately interconnected with emotion, and meaning springs from emotional engagement – particular books, films, theater, are all important to us because they connect with our own particular feelings.

Learning to read is an educational activity that should relate to a child's emotional life. If a child has a new baby in the home, for instance, it makes sense to read books about sibling rivalry, thereby drawing the child into the emotion and drama of literature, by dealing with something that is of importance to the child. If the classroom has a lot of immigrant children, books about finding yourself in a new place would be very relevant. This approach of following the child's emotional life allows the child to understand that literature is not just a boring subject in school but a way of connecting to the world and to others. If a child comes to know that the writer, and the teacher, understands or even shares his deepest feelings, including the negative ones, then he is more likely to become involved in and feel committed to the group. And his life long interest in literature begins.

Bruno Bettelheim, noted child psychologist, feels strongly that literacy develops through a child's emotional engagement, through motivation. The relationship between the child and the text, he believes, is the most important factor in developing literacy. In his book "On Learning to Read," he criticizes the authors and proponents of the dreary and meaningless stories presented in children's textbooks:

> By rendering an entirely monochromatic picture of what the child from his own experience knows to be most complex relations, feelings, and events, the stories are robbed of all deeper significance. Completely absent are the ambivalences, jealousies, anxieties, exaggerated and frustrated hopes that are the inseparable accompaniments of all deeply felt attachments and all truly important events.[9]

Although the average reading text has improved greatly since this book was written in 1982, the point itself is important: meaning and relevance are central to the acquisition of reading skills in a child's life.

Emotional safety in school

The feeling of emotional safety in the school environment is essential to involvement. Absence of a safe feeling leads to alienation from the group, and this is another important reason for integrating the emotions into the curriculum. Many teachers think it is their job to 'get on with the curriculum' or to prepare children for tests. Some feel they need to take charge of children, maintain control, and keep emotions out of the classroom.

A child does not feel safe in a classroom where there is a great deal of competition or focus on results, or the 'right' answer. If you are a high achiever, you may have to push aside your own interests and focus on what will please the teacher most, or what will gain you the most 'brownie points.' This child will not feel safe to take a guess, make a mistake, or let his mind wander creatively. A child who is struggling academically will also feel unsafe in this environment. He never takes a chance for fear of humiliation. He will never express true feelings because it may incur disapproval or even mockery, and compound his own feelings of inadequacy.

When a classroom teacher either engages in domineering behavior or suppresses a child's emotional life, she is not only inhibiting the child's emotions, but also his academic development. One of the negative consequences of being ignored as a sentient being is the tendency to exclude one's real self from the classroom and to withhold one's thoughts. When children do not feel involved in the school ethos, they are more likely to drop out of school.

Teachers who are well meaning and overly focused on 'results' due to pressure from their supervisors, can tend to fall into the trap of praising children who get the right answers. This can have a negative effect on children's emotions, and impact their cognitive development, BOTH the child who is praised as well as the child who never gets praise or can't ever come up with the answer the teacher wants to elicit. It's a pretty obvious fact, but not often taken into account, that there is more than one right answer. Some of the greatest geniuses of all time have been thought of as crazy because they questioned things taken for granted as true at the time. Teachers do nothing to encourage divergent thinking or creative insight when they adhere to 'the facts.'

Richard Quantz, who has written about rituals in society, and specifically schools, observed one pervasive pattern, which he calls the 'puzzlemaster' ritual. By this he means that in most classrooms the teacher sets himself up as a keeper of knowledge. During the course of the lesson he will try to elicit the 'right' answer from the pupils, who will be duly rewarded. Quantz points to this quizzing ritual as an indication of the decline of democracy within the school system. Children, he believes, are inculcated into the belief that the teacher is an expert who holds all the answers, and they themselves passive recipients of learning.

While we might theoretically advance the idea that schools are arenas of democratic struggle, the day-to-day reality of the high schools that I visited found such discourse not only nonexistent, but meaningless.[10]

He abhors the extent to which schools have assimilated the corporate culture into their structure, to the extent that the focus is on productivity. Indeed, focusing on one's own performance, and competing with others, does not seem to be the best preparation for students to be participants in the community. The singling out of one child over another in the classroom can be seen as an inculcation of elitism, a neglect of the multiple intelligences of children, and a failure to build a group ethic. In these ways, competitive schools and schools that teach only to achieve high tests results can be seen as failing to develop notions of citizenship in their students.

The dangers of competition

When children receive praise in relation to others, not only the relationship of children to each other but the health of the group as a social unit is damaged. Children need to feel approved of in relation to their own goals, which of course can also be the goals of the teacher, but they should not be approved of insofar as they compare and contrast with the achievements of others. Not only relationships suffer – a child's actual performance suffers if he has to work to a set of standards where other children's performance counts also. A child's motivation suffers when he feels compared with others – even for the child who excels.

Studies show that mastery praise is far more effective than social-comparison praise in terms of a child's academic work. A study done by Henderlong-Corpus examined the different short- and long-term effects of the different kinds of praise, mastery praise which validates a child's efforts in and of themselves, and social-comparison praise, which uplifts the child who outperforms other children:

Mastery praise benefits intrinsic motivation and social-comparison praise curtails it when uncertainty about children's subsequent achievements is introduced and, for girls, even in situations of continued success. Social-comparison praise arguably teaches children that personal competence should be measured by their relative standing in a group rather than their development of particular skills – a harmful message when children encounter situations that lead them to doubt their ability. Motivation and perseverance may be maximized, therefore, by avoiding social-comparison praise in favor of praise that emphasizes skill development.[11]

In other words, being compared to others damages not only the 'loser' but the 'winner', who is put in the position of constantly striving to be best, and this hyper-vigilant striving to outdo others negatively affects girls in particular. This study shows clearly that children in school should receive approval based on their own individual performance, rather than by comparison with others, because their emotions can interfere with their learning. If they feel they have to constantly be right OR they feel then can never be right, they will suffer either way.

Participation is an essential part of learning, and children who are afraid of being rejected or humiliated for their input will tend to not participate in the classroom. This is especially true of children with low self-esteem. Lack of trust in a social setting prohibits children from contributing positively to the group. A child who fears humiliation will be less likely to think of creative solutions than a child who is sure of acceptance.

Carl Rogers suggested that the three basic qualities needed to establish warm counseling relationships are **acceptance**, **genuineness** and **empathy**. This approach is the same one that teachers need to use, if they are to make children feel safe and ready to learn.

Emotional transference in the classroom

'Transference' refers to the way in which children and adults see others through the lens of their own experiences. For instance, a child who feels warm towards his mother will see the teacher as a warm accepting presence. The child who has a bully for a father will tend to see authority figures as harsh and may end up rebelling against all authority figures. A child who has a baby sister at home can get angry at a friend who takes the toy away because she experiences the same anger she feels towards her baby sister who takes her toys and her parents' attention. Transference plays an important role in the early childhood classroom, where children have not yet learned to disguise their emotions and readily act out their feelings on a regular basis.

Young children bring in issues to the classroom, such as sibling rivalry, or autonomy struggles with parents and re-enact them with teachers and peers. Older children can be struggling with serious issues in the home such as divorce or alcoholism, and, in the teen years this can play out in issues around self-esteem and body-image. Knowledge of the child's emotional life can make classroom interactions easier to manage and prevent a teacher from taking the child's emotional expressions personally.

A teacher who understands a child's background can adapt her techniques in order to make the child feel comfortable and develop better interpersonal understanding in the room. Her modeling of an accepting attitude can provide a positive role image for children to emulate, and in certain circumstances, a teacher may be the only positive role model a child has in his life. Many famous people who have made successes of their difficult lives attribute that success to one warm adult, a grandparent or a teacher who guided them along the way.

The frustrated teacher

In many U.S. classrooms, due to the pressure of the curriculum, many teachers do not feel able to be themselves. Ironically, teachers often become blamed for the boredom of children, when in fact they themselves are struggling to function within an oppressive system and maintain a sense of involvement in and commitment to their work. Boredom can set in when teachers are forced to adhere to a dull or repetitive curriculum. Teachers experience a huge amount of frustration because of the conflict between their desire to relate on an emotional level, and their inability to do so – most teachers get into the profession because they like children, not because they like their subject, and so they feel frustrated when they are not allowed to really help children.

Teachers are becoming more and more alienated from their profession. Teacher dissatisfaction is at an all time high, according to a Newsweek article in April 2015. The article states that:

> '*According to data from the U.S. Department of Education "enrollments in university teacher-preparation programs have fallen by about 10 percent from 2004 to 2012." In California alone, enrollment in teaching education programs declined by 53 percent over the past five years.*'

The article also states that not only are fewer people choosing to be teachers, but those who are in the profession are becoming more and more disillusioned, stressed, and ready to quit:

> 'The 2012 MetLife Survey of Teachers found that teacher job satisfaction declined from 62 percent of teachers feeling "very satisfied" in 2008 to 39 percent by 2012. This was the lowest in the 25-year history of the survey. The survey also showed how stressed teachers in America were. It found that over "half (51 percent) of teachers report feeling under great stress several days a week," an increase of 70 percent from teachers reporting stress in 1985'.[12]

The reason cited in the article is that teachers have lost control of the curriculum. More and more curricula are created by corporations, the article says, and teachers feel their individual creativity and ideas are not valued. That's understandable – if you feel like a robot then you are not going to experience job satisfaction. College graduates go into a nurturing profession like teaching with the hope that they can affect individual children's lives in a meaningful way. However, according to what we see around us, this is becoming less and less possible in a competitive, results-driven school system.

Regimented classrooms like we find nowadays in the United States leave everyone feeling drained and bored – pupils and teachers. An emotionally accepting classroom is a room full of life. Children may not be sitting in neat rows quietly working, or, if they are, then they are doing so because they are deeply involved in what they are doing. More often, happy, involved, busy and engaged children are moving, or standing, which is a more natural condition for children, and they should be talking to one another. According to A.S. Neill, psychotherapist and founder of the innovative Summerhill School and the concept of 'free school,' children are not quiet:

> 'Children are naturally noisy, and parents must accept this fact and learn to live with it. A child, if he is to grow in health, must be allowed a fair amount of noisy play.'[13]

Interpersonal learning is extremely important, and a busy classroom should have a nice, ongoing buzz of talk, a vibrant exchange of ideas, instead of a quiet hum of dissatisfaction or the silence of boredom.

The classroom

The dialogue and conversations that take place in an accepting classroom make the place vibrant, alive, and never boring. Though the noise is a negative side-effect, it may affect the teacher but does not appear to bother children in the same way. The stimulating effects of lively and honest conversation are important for developing literacy skills in children. If the teacher is careful to encourage even shy children to have a voice in the room, then interpersonal skills are developed along with language facility.

There are many benefits that accrue to society when schools allow time and energy to be disbursed to the important task of understanding and incorporating children's emotions in the classroom. One benefit is the development of a healthy mini-community, bonded by the empathy of a compassionate adult who regulates the group interactions and builds social skills such as anger management, tolerance, and reflection. This community can serve as a model for healthy social interaction later in life.

A second benefit is the release of children's natural interests and self-expressions. When a child feels comfortable in showing his or her interest in bringing in things to share from home and is enabled to follow those interests in the classroom, then real learning can occur, and these interests often spread to others in the room.

A third benefit is that, if the child's emotions are given a release, then he or she is less likely to act out these feelings on others, and more open to productive work. This release can be done through group discussion, one-on-one confiding in a teacher, or in healthy release mechanisms such as writing, dance, drama, or painting. These emotionally educational activities do not, in fact, take up long periods of time. All teachers are familiar with the child who constantly "acts up" and diverts everyone's time and energy from the work of the classroom. The amount of time spent on healthy "emotional work" pays off in terms of the kind of connection happy children make with their class work.

A fourth benefit of a tolerant and understanding classroom is that a teacher who understands a child's emotions can take control of a group with less energy than an authoritarian teacher might do. Children naturally respect authority figures who respect them and are anxious to please those who praise and encourage them. With this atmosphere, a teacher can accomplish more work than with a controlled one.

A final benefit of an emotionally accepting classroom is the satisfaction, which committed teachers will feel because of the effect they are having on young lives and the productive work they facilitate. Teacher retention would not be the problem it is today if teachers were allowed to do the job they probably thought they would be doing when they envisioned teaching in the first place caring for children.

Schools cannot continue to consider children to be intellectual beings, who leave their emotions outside when they enter the classroom. The emotions are an inextricable part of daily life. While most adults have learned to disguise or suppress their emotions in work situations, children have not yet learned to do so. If schools could play a role in developing children's emotional intelligence they might help to build a better society. Children in their own time could help create an environment where negative feelings are healthily expressed and not acted out in destructive ways in the public arena.

Chapter 3

A NEW DEFINITION OF INTELLIGENCE

Executive Function

Intelligence and how to measure it has been a topic of study for centuries. In 1912, a test called Intelligence Quotient, or IQ test, was devised by a German psychologist called William Stern. It was a scoring method for assessing certain skills, and it was rated on a comparison scale, so that people could know how their intelligence was rated against the scores of others. Another one of these kinds of tests is the Stanford-Binet test. It has been shown that IQ tests have variable results, impacted by age, stress, economic status, health, and so on. A person's IQ is not a fixed number and it is not genetically inherited.

In the 1980s a number of psychologists began to come up with a new theory of intelligence that is not skill-based. Donald Broadbent first proposed the notion of 'selective attention,' which means that humans can control their attention and direct it to that which interests them. Tim Shallice proposed the idea that there is a 'supervisory system,' which regulates attention. That means people can decide what is most important for them to focus on in any situation.[14] There are a complex set of skills which are associated with this philosophy of intelligence, commonly called Executive Function.

Executive Function implies that there is a driver at the wheel – a higher function that controls the other cognitive functions and directs them accordingly. Whatever kinds of skills a person has will be used in the service of the task that is decided on by the individual. The individual selects the task, depending on his or her priorities.

Exercising Executive Function means that a person can do some of the following important tasks:

- **Prioritize tasks.** Given a set of tasks, being able to know which one is most important, is a skill a child should be able to develop. A child who is emotionally evolved will be able to think about the value of the outcome of various actions. They learn this skill by being frequently asked to assess the outcome of their own actions and the actions of others. Being asked to recount what happened when you had a fight with someone, for instance, will help you to understand the narrative – the way one action follows another. By reflecting in this way, you will understand consequences in a way you would not if you were yelled at and made to feel ashamed. If a child understands the consequences of actions, he or she can decide what is the most important step to take in order to get to a desired result. He or she can prioritize a series of actions in order to achieve a desired result.

- **Pay selective attention.** In a complex situation, people should not panic. They need to be able to select out from the stimuli they are receiving in order to make good judgments. Children who receive emotional education are more likely to be able to remain calm and not be distracted by strong emotions in a stressful situation, such as a test, for instance.

- **Control emotions.** A child needs to learn how to keep emotions under control in order to achieve goals. Being able to understand his own emotions is necessary for a child before he can control those emotions. Emotional maturity means being able to know that it's important to plan an activity before you start it, rather than rushing. So if a child wants to bake a cake, for instance, he or she should look up a recipe first, then buy the ingredients, before starting the preparation.

- **Set goals.** Children who can set goals for themselves are high achievers. Setting your own goals is a higher form of cognitive function than adopting the goals of others. This does not mean that people can't go along with the goals of others, they can certainly incorporate and accept others' goals as worthy of effort. However, being able to set a goal for yourself and figure out the steps needed to reach those goals is a very valuable life skill and an indicator of Executive Function. Children in a school of Emotional Education will have enjoyed plenty of time in which they were allowed to write their own script, pick the cast, design the scenery, and so on, based on their initial goal of putting on a show. Much of their time will have been spent planning, as the teachers realize the value of experimentation and planning rather than 'cutting to the chase' and getting the show to look like something an adult would enjoy. In this way children develop an important skill and develop their ability to set their own goals and figure out how to get there.

- **Analyze input.** In order to make good decisions, children need to analyze the source of their information. Possibly the most important skill a child in a school of Emotional Education gains, is the skill of analyzing. Children constantly learn to think about **why** they did something, and **why** other people do things. This analytical skill is the mark of a high functioning individual. Being able to know why people do things informs us as to whether the information they give us is valid or relevant. For instance, a child will be able to judge that an ad for cigarettes is going to make smoking look glamorous, because it benefits the advertiser to do so.

- **Think flexibly.** A child should be able to adapt to surprises or unexpected situations. A person with low level Executive Function will think that doing the same actions will bring about a different result. A person who is not flexible will think that he or she should force through using the same techniques rather than imagining a new solution. But a child who is flexible will be able to adapt to new challenges in a fluid manner.

- **Monitor self-performance.** Children who have had Emotional Education will be able to analyze their failures and see where they went wrong. They will have learned this skill when teachers asked them to recount incidents and tell them in story form. They will have learned that they grabbed a toy because they felt jealous or insecure, for instance. This skill translates into self-monitoring and self-acceptance. If a child fails a test, he or she will be able to take a hard look and see what went wrong rather than reacting emotionally.

• **Project success for the future.** Children with narrative skills can come to understand that past actions lead to present consequences, and he or she can change the narrative for future improvement. First someone grabbed a toy, then I got angry, these are the beginning and middle of a story. The child can complete the story by adding a final chapter: I will not get angry the next time. Having the ability to construct personal narrative helps you to shape your future. Children with strong narrative skills can change their story and resolve conflicts more easily than those who can't see the patterns in their own actions.

Chapter 4

EMOTIONAL EDUCATION HOW DOES IT WORK?

Emotional Education is an educational program, which takes place during the regular school day, alongside the many other activities of the school program. There are two aspects to it.

The first technique is **Spontaneous Emotional Education.** While children are playing, learning, working on academic subjects, their emotions are always active. Teachers should accept and respond naturally to the natural expression of emotions during the course of the day. An academic program can operate fully alongside a program of Emotional Education.

The second technique is **Structured Emotional Education.** These are scheduled moments when the teacher sits with the class or with an individual child, or group of children, and works on a particular issue. This can be at circle time, or can take place during snack time or at any moment during the day. This can also be done in the form of creative homework assignments or projects children work on in groups independently.

Spontaneous Emotional Education

Everyone has feelings, the teacher, the individual, and the group itself. In an emotionally aware classroom, the program of A.R.T., which will be described below, allows for an open exchange between everyone about how they are feeling, on an ongoing basis, during the course of the day. Free expression of emotions should be allowed, even when working on projects. Sometimes it is NOT appropriate to stop and focus on feelings, let's say while crossing the road to the park, or on the staircase, or in the middle of a fire drill. But most times it is appropriate to address feelings, and sometimes it is absolutely essential to do so. For instance, two girls are arguing at the back of the reading group, and a teacher is distracted. The teacher can reprimand them, demanding that they be quiet, threaten consequences and so on, and this will be tiring to the teacher. It will put an end to the behavior, but not to the problem. The conflict still exists, it's just gone underground. In an emotionally responsive classroom, the teacher can have the freedom to stop and address the emotional distress rather than trying to keep it quiet.

The fight itself can become a mini-lesson, and can actually lead the group towards reading another book, which may be relevant to whatever conflict was going on. Just a note here to allay a teacher's fears about 'wasting time.' In the first place it is not a waste of time, it's like investing money earlier rather than later. It pays off in terms of saving problems from escalating and creating greater problems in the future, since it gets to the root of the issue. In the second place, emotional competence sets in with a group of children, so that once a group becomes accustomed to sharing feelings, it does not take long for issues to be resolved, so that for the long term it actually saves time and energy as well as helping children to develop self-awareness and social skills that will be useful to them.

Being emotionally responsive is like riding a bike, it may be time-con-suming at the beginning, but once the technique is learned, this kind of work becomes a matter of habit. Teachers and children will become more and more comfortable with sharing, once trust is established. As the year progresses, teachers can build on previous experiences and incidents. For instance, a teacher who is working in this way with children will have a store of ideas based on what has gone before. When there is a problem, she can say: "Yes, this is the same feeling you had last week when you and your friend were arguing during our reading lesson, remember? I think it's the same thing we talked about. What do you think is going on with you two now?"

Structured Emotional Education

There are structured or scheduled teaching moments in a classroom, these moments are used to build on the various moments of emotional learning that occur during the day and to clarify any issues that have not been resolved. At circle time, at lunch, during specific points in the day or the week, the teacher will teach about emotions, using various techniques. These emotional teaching moments will help children make connections – between their own feelings and their behavior – between other people's behavior and their presumed emotions – and between their own past, present and future behaviors.

The teaching sessions may consist of: sharing feelings in a group, acting out dramas, puppet shows, vocal exercises, musical expression, reading stories, writing exercises, discussing short videos, and so on, depending on the teacher's imagination and talents. They may consist of having children discuss emotional issues at home as a kind of homework. For instance they can find out what things their parents were scared of as children, what are parents' most proud or most embarrassing moments, what are parents' pet likes and dislikes, favorite memories, and so on, thus building family core values and shared narratives. Teachers can send home emotional games for parents and children to play. For instance parents and children can talk about: ten things I liked about today, and ten things I didn't like about today.

Mindfulness

Daily mindfulness or meditation practice can be very helpful to children. A teacher can create a quiet moment where children can learn to experience their inner selves. This daily practice strengthens the child's reflection 'muscle.' Meditation – which can be as little as 2 minutes or as long as 5 depending a child's age – has a lot of benefits for children:

1. A mindfulness session helps a child to take a break from the constant flow of emotions they experience.

2. A guided meditation can bring a child to awareness of feelings that may be going on inside.

3. Mindfulness and meditation strengthen the child's reflection 'muscle.'

4. Children who regularly meditate experience a relaxation of tension and develop lifelong skills of self-soothing.

5. Open discussions about problems and conflicts after meditation can be very productive.

WHAT ARE SPECIFIC SKILLS TAUGHT IN EMOTIONAL EDUCATION?

The program is designed to help a child feel emotionally safe in school, and to learn more about his or her feelings. The goals of the program are: to help children to gain understanding of and control over their own feelings, to give children insight into the feelings and motivations of others, to teach children coping mechanisms when deep feelings arise and to guide children towards healthy communication of feelings – both sharing and listening.

Children develop a set of skills in a school where Emotional Education is practiced. Very young children benefit from this program, and older children can practice these skills during the many years where they encounter different challenges, social and self-identity problems, and family crises. Over the period of time spent in school working with their emotions, children will learn to:

IDENTIFY their emotions and name them. If a child can identify feelings, then he or she can manage them. Knowledge is power, and being able to see yourself from the outside and know what you are feeling gives you the pause you need to make a calm decision.

COMMUNICATE their emotions in healthy ways. If a child can communicate emotions in a healthy way, she can avoid misunderstandings and conflicts, and make good connections with other people. Children relate well to other children who are open and communicative, and open and honest children tend to make good leaders.

RECOGNIZE patterns of emotional response in themselves. If a child can recognize patterns in himself, he can gain perspective on the kinds of decisions he makes. He can then change the script for his life and make different choices. If a child knows he gets sad whenever his mother drops him off to school, but doesn't get sad when his father drops him off, that is useful information for him. He can come to anticipate those emotional swells, and handle them better when they occur.

ANALYZE the reasons behind their own emotions. If a child can analyze the reasons behind her emotions, she can feel relief from the pain of having to experience negative feelings – knowing what's making you angry, for instance, can help you to avoid the need to get angry every time you confront a certain situation.

UNDERSTAND the motivations and emotions of others. Being able to understand the motivations of others will help a child to handle difficult social situations. For instance, if a child is being bullied, he can come to recognize that the bully has emotional problems, possibly stemming from his own family background. Knowing that others have problems will help a child to feel empathic and will encourage him to share his own difficulties, rather than engage in bullying.

EMOTIONAL EDUCATION

Chapter 5

THE TEACHER AS ARTIST

A huge part of Emotional Education, is of course, the care and maintenance of the teacher. Children learn through relating. The more they relate to their teacher the more they will learn from her. The more they feel the teacher's understanding and empathy, they more trust they will have and the more they will be open to discovering through his guidance.

The philosophy described in this book is called A.R.T. – Accept, Reflect, Teach. But the word ART itself is an apt description of what goes on when a teacher teaches. A good teacher is an artist. What does that mean? Here are some qualities of an artist:

THE QUALITIES OF AN ARTIST

Values feelings, intuition, inner experiences
Has a strong vision about how the world could be
Is flexible and open to change
Is comfortable being uncertain
Has a sense of wonder
Likes to explore new ideas
Is able to improvise under pressure
Is resourceful
Learns from others

Is in touch with a source of energy inside the self
Is interested in growth and self expansion

These are also the qualities of a great teacher. A teacher in a school of Emotional Education is able to IMPROVISE, a very valuable skill, as you will see from some of the stories that follow. He or she can tolerate uncertainty and relax, knowing that a good solution will present itself if he or she first accepts the problem.

It is very important that the teacher be supported in this work. The teacher needs to be given the freedom to make decisions, the validation in trusting her instincts, and the coaching needed in order to grow and develop these instincts. In many countries teachers are treated with respect and allowed to make decisions. In other countries teachers become mere puppets enforcing lessons and directing tests. These are not good practices and they lead to teacher boredom and frustration, and of course this trickles down to the children who are also oppressed and stifled.

Good schools allow for teachers to have autonomy and grow their creativity. This freedom has a beneficial effect on children. In Finland, where teachers are highly respected and allowed to develop their own ideas, children are reaching very high standards, and perform better than almost any country in the world.

Staff development workshops provide an opportunity for staff to share their own negative and conflicted feelings and get support from their colleagues. They also provide an opportunity to discuss the day-to-day experiences they encounter with children. This sharing is very productive and energizing.

Chapter 6

THE A.R.T. METHOD

The keystones of the Emotional Education system are the A.R.T. principles. The A.R.T. system means to:

ACCEPT

REFLECT

TEACH

These principles are the basis of the Emotional Education system in school, but they are also the basis of any interaction in which an adult engages with a child, in order to deal with emotional situations. The two principles of acceptance and reflection are in fact the basis of fair and healthy human interactions, and should be the underpinning of all our emotional engagements with others in our lives, whether adults or children. The point of using this system while communicating with others, is to avoid knee-jerk reactions and defensive or aggressive acts that can destroy relationships and alienate others. These techniques of acceptance and reflection are the healthy ways in which we can open our hearts, first to our own humanity and secondly to the humanity of others.

Teachers use the A.R.T. technique in school during regular interactions with the children and also in specific guided teachings. By using these techniques they are also modeling for children how they themselves can accept their own feelings and the feelings of others, and reflect them back to other people rather than reacting emotionally. So the program is for use by teachers in order to help children gain control, but it is also a model for children to use in their interactions with others.

Accepting the feelings of others and **Reflecting** back to them what we perceive about their feelings or what we honestly feel, is an incredibly productive way of interacting with another person. You cannot go wrong, you cannot get sucked into meaningless arguments, you cannot hurt others unintentionally if you stick to this method of accepting and expressing feelings. The third element of **Teaching** is essential when helping children to understand and manage their feelings, and modify their behavior in order to make themselves understood. This teaching is done in retrospect, after the emotions have subsided.

ACCEPT

There are two aspects of accepting – accepting the child and accepting our own reactions to the child.

Part 1. Accepting the child.

A teacher needs to be able to look at a child's behavior, no matter how frightening, repulsive, or socially frowned upon, and accept it for what it is. It might be a child having a temper tantrum, or a child hitting another child, or a child being destructive with toys. In the moment of accepting that 'this is really happening' the teacher will take time to gather her thoughts and tell herself that yes, if a child is, for example, being aggressive, then it is a fact that children are naturally aggressive, children do feel anger, children do feel the impulse to hurt or destroy, those are basic untamed feelings which come with the territory of being a child.

The teacher will accept that aggression is a human trait, which evolved for survival. In that moment of acceptance, the ground is laid for real change. If you do not accept something, you will be preparing to fight it or run away from it, and so you will not be able to help the child to understand what is going on inside.

Many people – teachers and parents – may think it is their job to 'fix' a child. They may believe that when they see something negative they should rush in and put an end to it, that it is their duty to do so. But with the A.R.T. system, the idea is that the only way to handle a problem is to first accept it. A teacher must be able to feel comfortable with uncomfortable feelings. While it is the goal of A.R.T. to educate children about the need not to hurt others and to engage in healthy communication, there is no rush to fix children's behavior in the heat of an emotional moment.

This method attempts to create a long lasting solution rather than controlling a child and having a 'quick fix.' This long lasting solution works, because it directs a child towards an understanding of his behavior, and that is the way he can have self-control.

Part 2. The adult accepting self

Not only should a teacher accept that a child is capable of negative emotions – a teacher must look inside and accept that he or she is also capable of having negative feelings – to be human means to have feelings. For instance, a teacher may see a child hit another child and this might make her feel angry. Maybe she remembers her older brother hitting her. A teacher may hear a child say she hates her lunch, and he may feel sad, or envious. Maybe he remembers that his parents couldn't afford a proper lunch when he was little. This might make him feel envious that the child has a lovely lunch and she doesn't know what it feels like to be hungry like he did.

Sometimes, before a teacher can accept a child's situation, she needs to accept her own negative feelings, which we all have, for instance feelings of annoyance, disappointment, envy, sadness, frustration. Though they happen to us all day every day, negative feelings are uncomfortable feelings. Those who are in charge of children often feel they SHOULD NOT feel sad or angry. They beat themselves up and think they SHOULD BE NICE all the time. That is not humanly possible, and a teacher must be kind to himself and take that moment to feel empathy for his own self, to feel his own feelings and tolerate the fact the he is human.

That very important PAUSE of acceptance allows a teacher to recognize the feelings, in order to prevent them being acted out in the moment. When we pause we experience a stillness. In that moment of stillness a feeling of peace can arise, where we realize – YES I feel lonely, YES I feel angry, YES I feel envious. And in that stillness our creativity kicks in – we can think of a solution to our pain. It might be a joke, it might be an expression, it might be a memory, anything which will help us deal with the situation in which we find ourselves. But the one thing that does not work is a knee-jerk reaction, because acting out is never a good solution. Pause, slowing down, reflection, is always the best way.

REFLECT

After the moment of PAUSE happens, when the teacher accepts the child's behavior as a negative expression of feelings, and accepts that she feels a certain way about it, then she can gather her thoughts and think how best to let the child know that she sees, and understands. Perhaps two boys are fighting over a toy. Or a girl is showing negative feelings towards her lunch and refusing to eat.

The teacher may initially feel alarmed at either of these scenarios, but she should stop and allow herself to accept that what is happening is just a normal expression of some emotion. Once she pauses, then she can begin to reflect. The teacher can say descriptive things to the child, like:

- John's face is getting red
- I think John might be angry
- Robert took the toy John wanted
- I think that is why John is angry
- Susan, I notice you are not eating your lunch
- I think you don't like that lunch
- I think you are disappointed because you wanted something different and you did not get it

It sounds very simple, it is a way of stating the obvious, and though it may seem redundant to an adult, for a child it is very important. What it does is gives a child an outside view of the situation, and that brings her outside of the emotions, to rise above, to see herself or himself in an objective way, like looking at a story. That is ALL the teacher does during this part of the process. This is NOT the time for a teacher to say things like:

- You don't like your lunch BUT your mother made it for you with love so you should be grateful.
- You're angry at him BUT you shouldn't hit it is not nice to hit and you should say you're sorry.

There should be NO BUTS ABOUT IT. The chances are good that a child may already know he shouldn't hit, he probably knew that before he hit but he couldn't control himself. Similarly the child may know her mother made the lunch with love, but that does not help her to stop feeling disappointed. At this point in a child's development it is more important that she understands the reason for her action, it is not possible or desirable at this stage for her to think about how someone else feels. That will follow shortly.

Put yourself in a child's position and imagine how dismissive it is when someone does not understand how you are feeling in a bad situation. For instance imagine that you just lost your wallet with a lot of money in it. You tell your friend. She says: "That's terrible! But you'll get more money. Besides, other people have worse things happen to them." Chances are this does not help you at all, it might even make you really angry. That's not the response you need right now. You need someone to accept how bad it feels to lose your wallet, and you want someone to understand how you are feeling. You don't need cheering up and you don't want your feelings compared to someone else's, or told that your feelings should be pushed aside, or told to 'get over it.'

A child should be allowed to experience feelings without being distracted, because feeling your feelings and fully knowing why things hurt is the only way to prevent yourself from acting them out. Many people try to distract children from feelings, and that is not a good idea. A child should be allowed to have feelings and have someone see and hear the expression of feelings, someone to witness them, and understand those feelings. These are the most helpful things an adult can do: see, understand, and reflect that understanding back to the child.

Making judgments and giving suggestions will not help a child who is overwhelmed with strong feelings. In the heat of the moment all a child feels is deep disappointment that there is peanut butter and jelly when she was imagining a bagel and cream cheese, or deep anger because someone took away a toy he wanted with all his heart and soul, and believes he will never ever have again, because that's the way a child feels and thinks.

Children have intense feelings, and when adults do not understand, children often feel deep injustice at how unfair the world can be when you are little and have no say in anything. These feelings can compound over time if they are not resolved in childhood and we all know the damage resentful angry people can do to others if they grow up with those childhood wounds unresolved. Peanut butter and jelly is just a small example, but the principle is the same no matter what the 'injustice' is – recognize, validate, and you take the sting away.

Being authentic and responsive

Being real in your interactions with children is a key part of the work of educating them in regard to their emotions. Here are some reasons:

- Children always know how a teacher or parent is feeling, no matter how we try to cover it up, they are very instinctive about recognizing emotions – it's probably a basic survival tactic that we have from birth. It is scary to a child when an adult is angry, and masks the anger with fake sweetness. A very good book to read to your child is: "Harriet, You'll Drive Me Wild!"[15] a book in which a mother tries vainly to mask her annoyance with sweet phrases such as 'darling child' through gritted teeth, until she finally snaps. (Don't worry there's a happy ending when everyone hugs!) Children love reading this book because it helps them to understand why, and how parents mask their anger. At the end of the story the mother explains to her daughter why she 'exploded.' That is a wonderful lesson for children who may find adult behavior confusing. It is better if a parent or teacher shows her anxiety, frustration clearly and simply in a non-threatening way.

- Children need to see how adults express feelings in non-threatening ways so they can learn to do it themselves. They feel distanced from a teacher who says: "Come on hurry up now, that's not the way to walk, I don't understand your slow feet." They can learn more from a teacher who says: "Oh no, I'm feeling worried that we will be late back to school. The pizza is going to arrive at 12 and the pizza guy will be waiting for us." They may feel confused when a parent says: "Sweetie, we talked about the wall – no climbing feet today." They will be more likely to understand and comply with a parent who says: "I wish you'd stop climbing on that wall, I'm so worried you'll fall." What they learn from this honesty is that adults have feelings, feelings they can relate to. It normalizes negative feelings and shows them that adults have to work on understanding and managing their feelings too. Children respond much better to an adult who shares feelings, than to a nagging or pressurizing adult. When you are not real about your feelings it comes across as nagging.

- Children particularly need to see how adults cope with negative feelings. Everyone has feelings and no one can get through a day without showing them. A teacher can be honest and say: "You know I am sorry I yelled just now but you weren't listening and I thought you were not paying attention. I just wanted you to hear my story. It was wrong of me to raise my voice like that. Did it scare you?" That kind of relating to children is respectful and helpful. In fact it will bring more safety into the room when a child sees that a teacher is willing to expose her real feelings and be humble in this way. Trust and mutual respect grow when people are emotionally honest.

- Children need to learn how to pattern their own adult behavior. When they get into relationships in later life, they will need to know that families can show the full range of feelings since they are all trying sincerely to communicate, not to hurt each other. Being in a family where people keep their feelings to themselves may make a child feel that she is weird just because she feels sad, or angry, or anxious.

- Children need to know that their presence and their behavior has an effect on other people. It is disrespectful to a child to pretend that you do not have a feeling in response to his behavior, or to pretend that nothing he does can bother you. Pretending you are not fazed when a child does something bothersome helps some times if you are in a public situation and don't want to react, but if it is your usual response to your child to ignore his behavior, then it can be very detrimental. Ignoring a child is tantamount to saying he does not matter to you, and some children may even act up just to get attention. Giving a real reaction to a child is very important.

- Children need to know that adults are human – they can fail, they can make mistakes, they feel, they are alive. It validates their own feelings and it makes them feel part of the human family. Showing authentic shock, weakness, annoyance, helps a child feel even safer.

When I started teaching, I was so intent on my agenda of conducting a lesson that I thought it was what mattered most. For instance, if I was reading a story I was horrified if the book accidentally fell out of my hand. I would feel like a failure. I would think: "Oh no, I can't even hold the book up, the children will feel I am incompetent if I don't do it perfectly, what kind of teacher am I…" Over the years I have learned that if the book falls out of my hand the best thing I can do is to react with a startled look and a "what just happened?" expression, because children will laugh uproariously. Laughter is their recognition – 'that's just the kind of thing that would happen to me' is what they are thinking, and that's why they laugh. They get it. Mistakes happen to us all, and we can laugh at ourselves.

Being able to laugh at our own mistakes as teachers is very gratifying to a child, a huge relief to ourselves, and it draws us all closer. When a mistake happens and I react to it, the children love it so much they ask me to do it over and over again, each time I act surprised is as funny as the first time. From this example, it's an easy matter to deduce that children love to see an adult failing and reacting honestly to that failure. They love to see adults making fools of themselves, and they trust adults who can laugh at their own folly. Being humble enough to show you can make a mistake is actually a sign of strength. Covering up your reaction does not help children because it shows them you are afraid of failure and have a weak ego. It helps a child to see a real reaction, because it validates their feelings. When I look surprised and annoyed at the book falling they know that this is what they would feel if they were in that situation.

Scripting and 'managing':

Some schools favor scripted responses and even coach teachers to use certain phrases. This is basically done to control the situation, and to manage children, which is the opposite of emotional honesty. Sometimes apologies are scripted, and some greetings are formalized. In one school, teachers are supposed to say 'I have a message for you,' before they tell a child something. And in some schools the teacher is encouraged to address the group all the time as "friends," rather than calling them by name. This scripting seems innocuous, but it has some not immediately apparent consequences.

Being required to address children as 'friends' distances the teacher from her feeling, it takes a child's individuality away, and it teaches children to think of themselves as expected to behave in a particular way, i.e. they are being asked to consider themselves to be the teacher's friends, or friends to each other.

There is of course nothing wrong with wanting everyone to be friends, but using this term as a matter of policy, implies that they are expected to be ONLY friendly, and children sometimes do not feel in a friendly mood. Children should be allowed the space and freedom to express negative emotions, because they are in school, and what better place than school to learn how to express feelings in a healthy way? School is the child's first experience of being in a larger group, and it's an ideal situation in which to learn how to relate to other people.

A child might feel angry and want to say: "She's not my friend! We just had a fight!" It would be better if she could express that, and have the teacher respond by asking: "Why not? What happened? Let's talk about that." This is more conducive to a child's well-being than acting as if there are no bad feelings, or that bad feelings have no room in school, they need to be kept to another place or dealt with at another time. A friend of mine was walking down the street with her four year-old son who attends our school. He said: "Mom, why is that lady always smiling? I don't like her smiling all the time." His mother answered: "I don't know why she smiles all the time." And her son said: "I bet she's angry at nighttime." I thought that was a good observation, and from a four year-old it seems like real wisdom. He knew that we can't all be happy all the time, it is not the way life works. Negative feelings are part of our lives and they should not be feared. In fact they should be paid a lot more attention, as they give us a clue as to what is going wrong.

Teachers are almost inculcated to 'manage' children and keep them under control, and that is very exhausting and unproductive in the long run. Teachers need to be supported so they don't have to think of themselves in this role. I remember one boy who was behaving badly at nap time every day. I knew he was having a hard time at home due to some domestic problems. I felt irritated that he kept making noise when others wanted to rest, I was annoyed that he kept deliberately doing things that were disruptive. I wanted to stop the behavior, and I thought that a good way to fix this problem would be if I tried praising him. So one day when he was being quiet I said:

"Thanks for being quiet Ralph, you are a nice boy." He seemed angry and he snapped at me: "I'm not a nice boy!" I knew immediately what he meant. He didn't want to be manipulated by me, or forced into a role, and he was right. I was trying to 'manage' him rather than being real with him. I corrected myself: "No, you are right. You don't have to always be nice. Sometimes you feel angry, like right now, and that's ok. I wanted to tell you that you are being quiet and that made me happy because I want the other children to rest. But it's also OK for you to be angry, and to feel that you don't want to be nice. You can talk to me and tell me whenever you feel angry, I will try to understand. For now though, it's helpful to me and the whole class for you to be quiet while others rest."

Our relationship grew stronger after that, and we had a good talks, I felt he looked at me differently now – he knew I understood him and I didn't want to manipulate him into being 'nice'. My mistake was in trying to correct the problem by giving him fake praise instead of being real. I could have said to Ralph: "I am irritated," or I could have said: "Ralph I am worried about the other children," or I could have said: "I wish you could be quiet," and it would have been more authentic, since those are all valid feelings. He called me out for my attempt to manage him, and I learned something. It is important not to manipulate children with praise or scripting. Being honest is the best way to gain a child's respect and cooperation. As a side effect, he actually did behave better at nap time.

In an emotionally accepting classroom, the teacher should not need to use scripting or ritual phrases in order to get children interested. I have heard teachers say: "put on your listening ears" and while this is not terribly wrong, it's physically not possible to do, we only have one pair of ears. For the teacher too, it's much better not to use scripted phrases to draw children into your plans. You can do it by showing them the activity and making it attractive for them. A creative teacher will draw the children into a group or activity in a way that is attractive or exciting – say a new project – without having to demand a specific behavior. That's the art of teaching, you have to be a performer in some ways. The activity itself, and the trust the children have in the teacher, will be enough to draw them together without having to tell them they need to pay attention.

For instance, if a teacher is starting a science experiment, he or she may even want to simply start doing the activity, pouring water, carrying out the sand, shaking a tub of pebbles, and even if all the children are not listening at first, they will be drawn in by the energy of the experiment itself. If there is a discipline problem, let's say the teacher feels the children are being silly, or that they are distracted, are intruding on each other's space, or any other issues which impede the teacher's agenda, and he can't get their attention, then he needs to be honest.

He can say: "I am trying to show you something interesting but I notice a lot of you are moving around and making noise, the rest of us can't hear. Maybe I will have to keep this fun activity for another time." In this way a teacher can show annoyance, frustration, etc. without getting hot under the collar or getting personal, and without covering up his or her feelings by pretending to be 'friends' when he feels irritated.

Teachers who are annoyed or worried about certain behaviors may say things like: "Use your walking feet," or "Hands are not for hitting." Both of these phrases are confusing, they are not fact based, they communicate little that is helpful to the child, and they are not very productive. You don't use different feet for walking or running – same feet in both cases. And hands actually are for hitting, among other things. You can hit a drum, or you can hit your friend, and one may be acceptable while the other is not, but it's simply not true that hands are not for hitting. Those are phrases which mask the teacher's feelings, and they hide the teacher's purpose from the child – they serve to control and manage, not to teach. Chances are these phrases get repeated over and over and no one grows in the situation.

A teacher should be honest with his feelings, OR just state the obvious. He could say: "People who run may fall," or "The floor is slippery, I am worried children will fall and get hurt," or "I know you're angry but it is not OK to hit. You can hit a pillow and it will help you get the anger out, but you should not hurt someone with your hands." The difference is that with scripted phrases such as 'use your walking feet,' or 'hands are not for hitting,' the teacher is in the difficult and ultimately futile position of controlling the child. Both teacher and child will end up frustrated. It's better to come out and say straight: "No, don't hit. It hurts." It's honest and it's clear and it is non-threatening.

Giving information and feedback to the child about what could happen and why it is wrong, will help the child to make decisions on his own. Telling a child that you are worried about the consequences of his actions is always better than nagging. The reason is that you are accepting responsibility for your own feelings rather than venting your frustrations on someone else. You share the fact that you are worried. That leaves open the question of whether the activity is right or wrong, whether the child can do the activity without getting hurt. You are worried and you want it to stop.

The child can respond that he knows what he's doing, there is no need to worry, or he can stop doing the activity so that he doesn't worry his teacher or parent. Generally children respond very positively to this kind of sharing of concern, and will stop their worrisome behavior.

Reflecting the situation to the child in a non-judgmental and non-threatening way helps him or her to make these decisions. If you see a child doing something that is very dangerous, you need of course to rush over and protect her. But if you see her about to do something that is potentially dangerous, you can also try to remain calm and say something that reflects the situation like:

"I see you are going to climb on the table. The legs of that table are pretty fragile. I'm not sure that they will be able to support your weight and it could collapse. That doesn't look safe to me, it is worrying me." If things like that are said in a calm voice, it will be much more effective than saying:

"Get off! Stop! What are you doing? You should know better! We don't do that in this house!" This kind of nagging creates anger and frustration, the child in fact does NOT know better and you can help her to learn about the world if you reflect to her the situation you see her getting into and reflect your honest emotions too. Letting her make the decision based on your advice and real facts gives her the opportunity to grow and become responsible.

NOTE: Of course a parent or teacher is ALWAYS entitled to forcibly stop a child from doing something dangerous if he or she continues to do it and you feel that the child may be reckless and likely to be hurt or hurt others. Adults have the right to have the last word in matters of safety.

TEACH

When a boat is rocking violently on a turbulent ocean, it is not the time to give lessons on how sea currents operate or what the structure of an engine is. The same is true for dealing with a child in the middle of an emotional situation – it's not the right moment to teach a child about codes of behavior, or how they are affecting others. The point at which the teacher should give a child information or perspective on feelings, is when the feelings are abated, the boat is in the harbor, and the situation is calm. Then the teacher can give examples and teach lessons to help instruct children about the various kinds of feelings, combinations of feelings, the universality of feelings, and so on. *Teaching should not be an attempt to fix.*

When an incident is over and the situation is calm, the teacher can teach about feelings in a 'teaching' way. For instance, a teacher might talk informally and instructionally at lunchtime when children are relaxed and eating. She can say something general and non-judgmental like:

> *Today some people were feeling angry. They wanted things that other people had. People sometimes get angry when they can't have things that they want. And sometimes people worry that other people will take away things that they want, and they'll never have them. It makes them nervous when someone grabs something away. And when people get angry, sometimes they do things that they shouldn't do, and they feel bad about it later.*

This is a non-confrontational and non-judgmental way to bring up an incident. And then once children don't need to feel defensive or ashamed, she can open it up for discussion.

"John you didn't mean to hurt Bob today, right, you just wanted that toy? "The teacher can even throw in a story about his or her own childhood, e.g. "I remember my baby brother used to take my toys and that made me angry too. "Normalizing feelings and letting children know that everyone feels the range of human emotion is very helpful, and is the opposite of shaming, which only makes a child feel alone and different from everyone else.

The teacher can guide children gently towards realizing that people have a reason for their intense reactions. She may know that there is a new baby at home, and that is why John is very upset when his toys are taken away. "Does your baby sister grab your toys at home, John?" she might say. At this point she is leading John to the recognition that his anger is not just at the other children in the class, but at his baby sister who has taken his crib, his stroller, his place on mommy's lap, and who now comes along and takes his toys.

Teaching in different situations:

Teaching about feelings can be done in different ways. Here are some ways in which the school of Emotional Education can teach children:

- In casual moments, during lunch, snack, sitting quietly, talking about feelings and reflecting on the day's emotions

- Reading books – relating a book to a child's experience, choosing books that relate to events in the classroom

- Acting out a story that children feel drawn to, maybe something that is scary that they want to replay over and over to master their fears

- Games such as role-playing, and reversal of roles, featuring issues that are going on in the classroom

- Sharing stories – a teacher can relate stories of his own childhood, or instances he has seen that illustrate certain emotional reactions people can have

- Training a child in voice management and expressive techniques

- Teaching social skills such as self-assertiveness, ways of making friends

- Teaching the child about the self – encouraging him or her to reflect on what kind of things make you an individual, what do you like, what do you hate, how are you different.

Summary:

A.R.T. means that an adult must first accept. That means taking time to accept not only what you see, but accept what you *feel* about what you see. Then as an adult you need to reflect what you see, gently and non-judgmentally, back to the child. And finally, you can teach the child about what happened, by working on lessons, formal or informal, that will help to guide the child towards understanding emotions.

EMOTIONAL EDUCATION

Chapter 7

PRINCIPLES OF EMOTIONAL EDUCATION

ACCEPTING

Creating a safe, accepting space
Accepting negative feelings in a child
Allowing conflict
Letting go of agenda
Refraining from judgment
Refraining from 'fixing'
Allowing and supporting emotional expression
Processing feelings at staff meetings
Accepting negative feelings in yourself
Understanding family dynamics that may affect a child's behavior

REFLECTING

Stating the obvious
Identifying feelings
Reflecting objectively what you see in conflict situations
Being authentic and responsive
No forced apologies

No redirecting away from feelings
No 'buts'
Narrating to the group what is going on
Feeling a child's feelings
Speaking empathically without judgment
Reflecting your own feelings where appropriate

TEACHING

Building emotional vocabulary
Explaining terminology and complex or conflicted emotions
Giving examples from your own childhood
Building group understanding through reflecting on conflicts
Putting on 'shows' to illustrate emotional situations
Identifying patterns by pointing out recurring themes
Building reflection in the child through questioning
Teaching good communication skills
Teaching the family
Building coping strategies
Empowering the child through vocal training

CREATING A SAFE ENVIRONMENT

Creating a safe, accepting space

Teachers must create an atmosphere of acceptance of emotions so children feel safe enough to show their real selves. A child enters school in the morning with a set of feelings. Teachers need to address each child's feelings (when necessary) in order to alleviate and unburden the child. Some feelings may be more pressing than others, and teachers need to know how to prioritize who needs attention and who would prefer not to have attention. Teachers need to STOP and take time to LISTEN, to acknowledge emotions rather than steamrolling over them. There are exceptions to the rule but in general feelings should always be attended to especially if a child appears distraught or depressed. Acceptance is expressed by:

A quiet demeanor

Teachers should allow children to cry, to be angry, to look shy, etc. without trying to change them. The child is showing him or herself in the initial encounter, and the greatest gift a teacher can do is to allow them to show this self without intrusion. At first a teacher should watch and wait, and create a quiet environment so a child can be safe enough to let these feelings show.

Breathing calmly, not reacting, allowing things to unfold, staying still, are all part of a teacher's tool kit. Trust takes a while to establish. Refraining from labeling a child is very important at this stage: " You're shy," is the worst thing you can say to someone who is being appropriately cautious in a new situation. It is enough to make a child feel reluctant to trust his own feelings.

Non-judgmental comments

Teachers can say things like: 'I wonder if you are feeling sad?' Or 'I notice a frown. I am curious if you are worried.' Or 'You seem angry to me because of the way you are standing.' All of these comments contain the word 'I' or 'me' and the implication of this is that the teacher accepts the fact that she is perceiving something, and may be right, or wrong about what she perceives.

A teacher should not make statements like: 'You are angry,' instead, she should say she notices something. There is a big difference between saying: "You are angry," and "I think you might be angry," or "I notice your face is red, I wonder if you are angry." The child may react in a number of ways, "No I'm not!" she may turn away to hide her face, or she may leap into conversation: "Yes I am so angry at Teddy he took my book," these reactions can be hard to predict and the teacher should be cautious not to label behavior until the child is in agreement.

Children often don't know what they feel, so the teacher should adopt an inquisitive or scientific tone. He can say: "Hmm I wonder if you are feeling sad or angry?" Children will be very honest – they will not make up answers to please adults. Trust them when they tell you the answer, and watch their facial expression, which will reveal the truth.

Supportive and non-judgmental phrases

A good response to any expression of emotion can be: 'I see.'
Or: 'Thank you for telling me, I wasn't sure.' Or: 'That must feel bad,'
Or simply: 'I know." These comments should be substituted for
suggestions on how to behave or ideas for soothing your feelings. They
are open ended. These phrases spoken gently and sincerely can make
a child feel very comforted and willing to share more. Teachers should
not jump in and say "Don't worry," or "Don't feel sad," or otherwise try
to change the mood. Allow the child to direct the mood.

Comments addressed to the group

'He's feeling a bit sad now, he might not want to talk, just give him
some time,' can let a child know that you understand his feelings and
you are willing to defend his right to have them within the group – this
can make him feel accepted and safe, and he will know he has an ally.

Chapter 8

EXAMPLES OF EMOTIONAL EDUCATION

ACCEPT

Accepting negative feelings in a child

There are many feelings that parents find hard to accept in a child. One of these is sadness. It is important for parents to be able to tolerate the sadness their child feels. When a parent can't tolerate his child's sadness, he may try to distract him or minimize the feelings. Here is a letter I send to parents at the beginning of the year when separation is difficult for children and for parents. The letter was also published as an article in Parents Magazine.[16]

The Beauty of Tears

As a preschool director, I see a lot of tears, particularly during the first few weeks of school. For the first time, children are going through an extended period of separation from their parents. This is a formative stage when a young child is beginning to learn that she can be part of a group outside the family.

During these transitional days, preschoolers begin to discover how to cope with separation, anxiety, loss and change. These are skills and techniques they will need throughout their lives. Finding resources within themselves and comfort in others is an important emotional task for children. While parents are naturally protective of their children, they often fail to realize that children have great resilience and access to coping strategies within themselves. It is our job to help them access that coping place.

One thing I have observed, is that children have easy access to tears, while most adults have lost their ability to cry when they are sad. Parents often cringe when they see little ones crying, and often try to stop them – even total strangers will intervene as though they can't bear to see a child cry.

In my opinion, however, tears are one of the best coping strategies. Children should be allowed to cry. Crying is a socially adaptive skill particular to humans, and it has many benefits.

Crying releases tension. Keeping feelings of anxiety, grief, anger or loneliness inside is like holding a beach ball underwater. If you are withholding sadness, you are probably holding your breath, your forehead is contracted, your shoulders are pulled up, and your body is rigid and on guard. Once you cry, your lungs expand and fill with air. Your face stops tensing and your muscles relax. When your crying bout is over, your breathing returns to a healthy rhythm and you are taking in slow deep waves of oxygen. After you cry, your eyes sparkle and your whole body feels rejuvenated.

Crying draws people to you. I have observed that the most popular children are the ones who show their feelings openly – everyone can relate. Other children often come over to comfort the crying child. They trust the child who cries because "what you see is what you get." Strong bonds are created this way.

Crying helps other people. When a child is too tense to cry, he or she can relate to the person who has cried and feel grateful that an unspoken feeling is being expressed. It shows the fearful child that he or she isn't the only one to have the urge to shed tears.

Crying tests the teachers. Children observe how teachers react to the tears of their friends. Once children see that teachers have passed the test, given hugs or encouraged the crying child to seek comfort from friends, they know they are in good hands so that they can feel safe to show their feelings also.

How Best to Handle Crying
Some children just want to be held and understood. They appreciate that someone knows what they are feeling. Parents and teachers can simply say, "I know how you feel." Even if they are crying loudly, children hear our words.

Some want to be left alone. These children might resist being comforted. They may prefer to stand in a safe place, such as partially hidden behind a piece of furniture. They sometimes go in and out of a crying bout, processing their feelings, spending time observing others playing, and then crying again, they keep their eyes on the teacher, but they don't want anyone, yet.

Other children have the urge to cry until they are unable to stop – and that is the time when we need to step in to help them find a way out. These children may need a fun distraction, a job helping the teacher, water or sand play, something sensory to focus on or make them laugh. This is not the same as distracting, these particular children just need a help finding some way of coping.

These are all individual styles of adjusting to change and separation, and they all need to be respected. One child may employ a number of these coping mechanisms. It is the teacher's job to analyze, respect, and support the child while he finds his own way of discovering a happy place.

What Not to Do to a Crying Child
Never tell a child, "Stop crying; you're OK." Also refrain from saying, "Crying will make your eyes red/make me feel sad/make you look bad in front of others." Don't try to distract your child from crying unless you have tried everything else and he is making himself agitated or uncomfortable.

All of these responses will make a child feel that crying is not OK, is embarrassing or painful for the adult, and they may make him feel that crying is not a valid response to a stressful situation. We want to normalize crying – to let a child know that everyone cries some times, and it is acceptable to cry. The more an adult is able to accept the child's tears and really stay in that uncomfortable moment, the quicker the tears will pass. A simple word like "Aww…" and an understanding facial expression can help in these situations.

To help children get through the phase of separation, we often read books about crying and separation. Children like these stories, as they enjoy the fact that the feelings are normal – if someone wrote about it then I am not alone! Children like symbolic representations and often play out their feelings in dramatic scenarios with toys. We can enter their play – create a little show about a bear who misses his mommy, and then let them take the lead in the story. They will use this technique to adjust to their new feelings and their new situation.

Parents also need to allow themselves to shed some tears. Letting go of your child for the first time brings up many deep feelings. Acknowledging our own emotions helps in accepting the tears of the child and recognizing the beauty in this wonderful coping strategy that makes us truly human.

Allowing conflict

One person can never fix another person's problems. Though this may sound hard to grasp, it is very liberating once you realize the truth of it. People cannot take each other's problems away or make decisions for them. A teacher cannot take control of a child's life, she can only guide, and support. She cannot take conflict away, she can only guide a child through it.

A teacher can be enormously helpful to children in letting them accept that conflict is natural. She can help a child to develop his or her own strategies of coping in situations of conflict when they arise. Conflict resolution is a term often used in school programs. However, conflict endurance is a much more useful skill to have. Being comfortable with feeling uncomfortable is a great strength. It prevents people from attacking when they feel conflict, it prevents people from backing down when they have conflicting feelings, and the path of discomfort often leads to creative solutions.

Children need to learn how to tolerate and give a name to uncomfortable feelings such as embarrassment, disgust, fear, loneliness, anxiety, and to understand that they may have two conflicting feelings at the same time – such as sadness and anger, for example, or desire and fear. When children are in conflict, it is important for teachers to allow them to fully understand what is going on between them, guide them to reflect on what each one is feeling, and help them come up with the words or gestures to express these feelings honestly. Teachers need to avoid blaming or shaming and to avoid creating victim and aggressor. Both children in any conflict need help.

A great mantra for a teacher to have when she sees children experiencing conflict is to just STATE THE OBVIOUS. Say what you see. Then see what happens. It is a form of magic.

Teacher, help!

Recently a teacher called Maya was sitting on the floor playing with trains with two children. On the other side of the room she could see a child called Julia getting into a tussle with another child over a doll. Blanche had picked up a doll that Julia put down on the floor. Julia grabbed for it, but Blanche pulled it out of reach. Julia cried out to the "Teacher, help!" with a needy look on her face.

At this point in the year, Maya knew that Julia had a habit of wanting her to take her side – whenever things went wrong she would try to get Maya to come in and get her the toy or book she was fighting over. Maya also realized something about herself. She realized that some part of her enjoys being needed by children, rushing over to help, sorting out their problems. It always gave her satisfaction to know that she could soothe, fix, take care of other people, part of why she enjoyed the teaching profession.

She loved when children reached out to her for help, her nurturing instincts were gratified. Now, however, Maya was stuck on the other side of the room not able to jump up and run over, and that distance gave her pause. She thought for a minute, she had a choice: she could jump and run over there. She could ask: 'Who had the doll first?' or say: 'Well you put the doll down, and she picked it up, that's fair.' OR she could let go of these solutions and try to let Julia solve the problem by herself.

THE SOLUTION:

Maya took a deep breath, and did not respond at first. Then she decided to just state the obvious:

"I see Julia is upset." (Here she paused, letting the words sink in, watching for any response.) Julia just stared at her. "I think Julia wants that doll, but Blanche wants it too. Is that what's going on, Julia?" Julia nodded. Maya just stood (or sat) her ground, resisted the temptation to go over to the two girls, and said:

"I see. That's what's going on. Two girls want the same doll. Hmmm. That's a problem. I wonder what we should do." By some miracle (which often happens!) the problem sorted itself out. Julia looked back at the doll. Then she looked at Blanche. And she let go.

Why it worked

While it doesn't always work that way – the conflict may go on and on – what does always happen is that the child gains PERSPECTIVE on the situation. And the teacher gets to stay out of the role of problem solver. Which is a bad role for anyone! So by STATING THE OBVIOUS, the teacher in effect is holding up a mirror to the child, and this role is much more conducive to having the child learn to solve her own conflicts. When a child sees herself from the outside, she often gains perspective on the situation and finds an appropriate solution to her dilemma. It is liberating to see yourself from the outside.

Teachers handling conflict in themselves

Teachers need to be able to tolerate discomfort in themselves. By the time they get to be teachers, they have often set up the expectation that their job is to make everything go smoothly. And to keep everyone happy. This is a terrible burden for anyone to place on themselves. When you are dealing with children the general rule is NOTHING GOES SMOOTHLY. Except when they are asleep, and that is not always true either. Teachers often have to unlearn lifelong patterns of trying to make everything go smoothly. Teachers can help children work through conflicts on their own. But first they must tolerate the conflict within themselves, and deal with the side of themselves that wants to fix things instantly.

The first step for a teacher is to tolerate uncomfortable feelings, to sit in them for a while, before making a decision how to act. Here is an example of a teacher handling her own feelings:

I want to pee standing up like the boys

Clara is almost three years old. At potty time the children are almost all toilet trained, and they stand in line and wait for the potty. They can see each other and when one is done the other one can go in. One day Clara says:

"I want to pee standing up." Jenna the teacher feels a mixture of feelings, which make her uncomfortable. She is wondering what she should do. The various voices in her head tell her: 'Girls shouldn't pee standing up,' 'If I let her do this she will want to do it all the time,' 'This will make a mess on the floor,' 'I'm the teacher I have to make the rules,' and then the other calm voice that says: 'But what harm is it?' 'Maybe she sees boys doing that and she wants to do it.' 'Why shouldn't she?' She hesitates, she can't decide what to do.

THE SOLUTION

Jenna is aware that she feels uncomfortable. Fortunately, she is aware that in our school she is allowed to make decisions based on her own judgment, she does not have to follow rules unless they make sense to her in the particular situation. So she takes a breath and says:

"OK. Go ahead." Clara manages to stand over the potty and pee. She does so without making the huge mess that Jenna anticipated, but there is a little mess. Jenna thinks. She does not want to punish or reprimand Clara, but she knows that Clara should realize that the floor is messy without making a big deal of it, as boys make a mess too when they are first potty training. She says:

"Look there's a little spill on the floor here. I will help you to clean it up. Sometimes that can happen." The next time Clara asks again.

Jenna lets her do it. After a few times trying to see what it's like peeing standing up, Clara decides that she would rather sit on the toilet.

Why it worked

Jenna discusses this issue with the other teachers at a staff meeting, and they make suggestions as to why Clara might have wanted to try this out. Maybe she sees her baby brother is a boy and gets a lot of attention. Maybe she is feeling 'penis envy.' Maybe she wants to assert her individuality and do things her way. One teacher pointed out that in many countries toilets are different, and people don't sit on them like we do, everyone pees standing up, so this is a cultural constraint. The other teachers agree that Jenna was right to be flexible and to rethink her own preconceptions.

This is a good example of why it's important to not react immediately. If Jenna had just reacted without thinking she might have said something like:

Girls don't do that....You will make a mess...It won't work...We don't do that here.

Those comments would have made Clara feel that she was not really listened to. She probably would still want to try her new idea, and might even have felt different from everyone else or ashamed.

Jenna was courageous enough to experience discomfort and acknowledge it, and not react, until she had come up with the solution that felt right. She went against everything she had been taught when she was a child, and made a good decision. In so doing she allowed Clara to make a choice, work it through, and come to her own decision about whether peeing standing up was for her. If she hadn't been allowed she might have held on to the feeling that had been prevented from trying something new. This way it's tried and done and she moved on.

* * * * * *

Parents handling conflict

People need to learn how to handle stress. You can't learn how to handle stress unless you experience it and find your way through it, with a little guidance and support. Parents should NOT let children get embroiled in conflicts and stressful situations and leave them all by themselves to figure their way out of it. However they should also not fix everything for children. Let's take an example.

Mommy She's Mean to Me!

Susan comes home from school and tells her mother she does not like a little girl in her class. 'Mommy she is mean to me,' Susan says. Her mother immediately feels protective, guilty for allowing her child to suffer. She feels worried, angry, helpless. She probably wants to change the world and put a wall around her daughter, so she will not have to suffer. She may do or say any of the following things:

- *Say: 'How dare she! I will call her mother right away.'*

- *Write a note to the teacher saying she does not want Susan to be anywhere near that girl*

- *Tell Susan to be mean back to the other girl, suggesting a few choice retaliatory phrases*

- *Tell Susan to stay away from that girl*

But none of those solutions will really help Susan. The mother should first ask herself how she feels about this story. Maybe it reminds her of being bullied in school herself, maybe she did not feel protected and she does not want that to happen to her child. How she feels is going to influence her reaction to Susan's problem.

Susan's mother needs to accept that Susan will have to deal with difficult people in life and she should prepare her for these situations. The best way for Susan to learn how to deal with it, is to first realize how she felt when the girl was being mean to her. She needs to remember her own reaction, to feel her feelings, and put a name on them. This is important because when it happens again she will know what she is experiencing, and she will have a sense of control. This self awareness will enable her to deal with the situation in a calm way. And secondly Susan's mother can give her some insights into how to handle herself.

Here are some helpful things a parent can do when a child brings home a complaint of being bullied or teased by another child:

- Ask what exactly the other child did in detail – this will help the child to analyze step by step what happened, and see it as a narrative

- Ask how it made the child feel – sharing the feelings and going over them again is therapeutic, and gives the child words for her anger, fear, frustration, etc.

- Ask the child if there was something they would have liked to say or do that they didn't say or do. They can say whatever they want, even if it's angry, it is a helpful expression of how they felt, a release of anger or sadness in a safe place.

- Ask the child: 'Why do you think that little girl would say (or do) something like that? Having the child realize that there must be a reason for the child's unsociable behavior will empower her and make her feel less like a victim.

- Ask their child for ideas about what they can do the next time this happens.

- Encourage the child to tell the other child how that behavior made them feel in the moment when it is happening, e.g. 'I feel angry when you do that' or 'that's embarrassing' or 'That makes me sad.'

- Tell the child that there are authority figures or peers who can help. If the child is being picked on, then she should tell someone who can step in and be of assistance.

These strategies help the child process the feelings, get a handle on why the other person behaved that way, and come up with strategies to handle them. The best weapon a child can have is to realize that the person doing the bullying has a problem, he or she is not a powerful figure she needs to be afraid of. Knowing that other people have problems and motivation for what they do makes a child feel less like a victim, she will be able to understand that there is nothing she did wrong, the problem lies with the other person. Asking a child to attack or ignore others does not help the child to feel supported. Dealing with conflict is a vitally important part of a child's education.

Letting go of Agenda

Teachers often think they have to complete a curriculum item, or play a controlling part when there is conflict in the classroom. Being 'in charge' is a role that a teacher assumes, and often he or she will have misconceptions about this role. A teacher's vision of his or her role might include the idea that he or she should always keep going once a lesson has started or a story is being read. This kind of thinking is not always productive, and can in fact make a teacher miserable, since it puts a huge burden on him or her to complete the task, no matter what comes along. If a teacher is allowed to let go of his or her agenda and improvise, there will be a lot more freedom and flexibility and less pressure and exhaustion.

Is this a joke to you?

It is meeting time in the 4s class. Joan is the head teacher, and she is sitting on the chair and doing the usual morning routine of greeting everyone, then talking about the job chart, selecting children for jobs in the classroom – snack helper, bunny feeder, bell ringer, etc. Children are sitting on the floor, watching the teacher and listening to find out what jobs they will have - they all love to have jobs and they take them seriously. The assistant teachers are sitting in the circle too, one of them has a child on her lap who was feeling lonely in the morning and needs a lap to sit on.

The other assistant teacher, Roger, is sitting in the circle too, keeping his eye on everyone and watching the head teacher for cues in case she needs anything. Each group of teachers works as a team in this way. Once the children's jobs are allocated, Joan moves on to talk about what they will be doing for the rest of the day, pointing at the schedule, and asking children which area they want to play in first, the dress up area, the block area, or the table toys. Two of the girls begin to push each other and it is distracting to Joan. The girls, Mary and Kate, seem to do this a lot, and the teacher is feeling a low level of apprehension because at times the conflict between them has been know to escalate, even to hitting.

Mary and Kate both have younger siblings, and both of the girls' parents are devoted but extremely busy working parents. Both Mary and Kate are the oldest in their families and both of them are treated as the responsible ones in the family, the ones who take over and care for the younger ones when they are asked. They are the kinds of girls who will do jobs in the classroom well, and they both love to help others.

Though they are good and helpful girls, they are also quite emotional, both of them, and they often get into tussles with each other, which teachers see as power struggles, or competitiveness. Neither of them likes to be told what to do, as older siblings they tend to be slightly dominant. And yet they can both at times regress easily to a childish state of bickering and hitting. Today the pushing is escalating, Joan asks them a couple of times to stop, and she does this quite gently and matter-of-factly, to minimize the disruption for the other children by not making a big deal of it, hoping it will just stop.

However, this time the disruption keeps going on and on. Joan makes eye contact with Roger, and he understands this means she needs his help with the problem. Roger comes around and sits down beside the two girls and gives them a stern look as if to say: 'I'm watching you, now please stop this.' They do stop for a long few moments, and then once more they begin pushing and suddenly one of them lets out a big squeal: "Ow she pushed me!" Joan looks at Roger and nods, which, based on the discussion the teachers had the last time they talked about the girls means: 'maybe you should take them out of the circle now.'

Roger says: "You two girls will have to leave the circle now." They are both angry and don't want to leave, they give Roger dark scowls, but he shows them his serious face and points them out of the room. Roger brings them to the reading area just outside the room and the two girls stand close together with their heads down, looking sheepish, while Roger stands over them, getting ready to have a serious discussion about disrupting the circle time again.

"What's going on with you two?" he asks. "I thought we talked about this before?" Suddenly the two of them begin to laugh and giggle and look at each other but not at Roger. They nudge each other and the more Roger tries to be serious the more they laugh.

"Pay attention!" he says. He is feeling very angry now. "Do you know why you were taken out of the circle?" he asks. They giggle some more. They look at each other and completely ignore him and they seem to gain strength from each other's support. Roger feels like his blood is boiling. He is losing control. They are laughing so he can't do anything at this point to make them feel responsible for their bad behavior. "Is this a joke to you?" he snaps. They are silent for a moment and then they laugh even more. Now Roger is left standing there not knowing what to do. He feels helpless and angry.

THE SOLUTION

Suddenly Roger feels he is facing a blank wall. Getting angrier is just not going to help things move forward. It will only make them laugh more. He is going to look more and more foolish and they are going to keep on laughing. The situation seems ridiculous to him, insoluble. He knows he is stuck. And in that moment he realizes that since nothing is working, he has to let go.

And when he lets go of his current tactic, he realizes that yes, it is funny. It is a joke to them. They are laughing together, and he sees that now they are not being mean to one another. THEIR anger is gone, just like that. He asks himself: Why am I angry when they're not? He looks at them and sees that they are not fighting any more they are actually best friends, and so he says:

"Are you friends again?" and they both jump up now and give each other a big hug. Roger knows that he has to let go of his anger as quickly as they let go of theirs. At that point he decides there is no point in going on about this, it's best to just move on. If everyone is happy then why not go with that? At another point in the day, maybe when they are eating lunch, or at quiet reading time, he will take the time to say to them:

*"You two are such good friends, but you fight sometimes, right?"
When they agree, he might ask them what they like about each
other, and that is enough right now to guide them on the path
towards self-reflection. Clearly he is not going to change their
behavior in a major way in just one encounter, so it is best for him
at this point just to get them to see that they do have things in
common. In this way they will build a bond with each other. When
the bond seems strong between them he might guide them by
saying something like:*

*"What was it that bothered you today at circle time?" and get them to
articulate what it was. But that is work for another day. Right now
it's enough for Roger to realize that you don't always have to make a
big deal of problems, and you don't have to stay angry. He has
learnt from children that feelings come and go and it is fine to switch
gears and not hang on to a negative feeling if the moment has
passed. There is always time later to discuss feelings, when every
thing is calm.*

Why it worked

This solution worked because once again the teacher realized he was
caught up in feelings. He was picking up the conflict and internalizing it,
and trying to resolve it. He became aware of himself, and what he was
feeling, and this enabled him to step outside and see himself
objectively. Suddenly, when he realized what he was doing, he saw the
absurdity of it.

The children were moving on, and he needed to follow their lead.
Some situations call for analysis, for discussion, for heart to heart talks.
Some just need to be laughed off. "You had a fight? It's over? Good!"
End of story. Letting go is good. Life doesn't have to be so fraught.
Another day there will be time for analysis.

✳ ✳ ✳ ✳ ✳ ✳

Allowing and supporting emotional expression

Letting children say what they are feeling is a great gift to them. This supportiveness can help a child grow in confidence.

I'm so angry with you!

It was an art class in a 3-year-old classroom, a rainy afternoon with the lights on, and everyone was in a busy mood, enjoying the work. I set the children an assignment to take red and blue stickers and make designs with them. They could make patterns, or shapes, whatever they liked, then take a marker and connect the shapes, whatever came to mind. Everyone was happy and busy. I walked among the tables and pointed at the children's work as I went. I was so pleased that they liked the exercise and were busy and involved.

"That's lovely, June!" I said. "Yours is really nice, Oscar." I moved around the group. "Margot, that's great. That purple looks good with the red layered on top of it." Suddenly there was a growl from another table.

"I'm so angry with you Eileen!" said a sweet little girl called Hannah, her elbows on the table, her face filled with anger. I was surprised. What had I done? I walked over to her.

"You're angry with me, Hannah? Why? What did I do?" I asked. "You didn't say anything about my picture!" she scowled. "I see. You think I didn't notice you." I said. "I see why you are angry. Actually I didn't get a chance to come over to your table yet, that's why I didn't say anything. But yes, I know how horrible it feels when the teacher doesn't seem to notice you." She seemed glad to hear this. "Some children think that the teacher doesn't see them when she's not looking right at them." I said. "But I am very proud of you actually, that you could tell me how you felt. It's not easy to tell a teacher you are angry at her. I am glad you could say that to me and not feel afraid." There was a pause.

"I'm angry with you too," another voice said shyly. "You didn't look at mine either." I laughed inwardly. I could tell that this other child was not really angry like Hannah had been, he was smiling, enjoying saying these words to the teacher, and hoping to get praise just like Hannah had. I felt good that these children could practice with an approving adult, and learn that they can be allowed to say what they are feeling. Soon they were all having fun telling me they were angry at me, and we had a good laugh.

Why it worked

In this situation, many adults might be upset at the idea of a child saying they are angry. They might even say something like:

- Don't dare say you are angry at me, I am your teacher/mother/father

- Don't speak to me in that tone of voice, be polite!

- You're not angry

- Don't make a big deal out of something small

- Why do you always need attention?

- It's not important whether I like your painting or not, you should tell yourself that you like it

- You need to be more patient

Why do some adults react like that? Many adults can't tolerate anger in children – it frightens them, they wonder how they are going to control it. They think that if they acknowledge it then the child will be even more angry in the future, they think they are going to open a Pandora's Box.

However, that is not true, the opposite is true. The best way to handle a child's anger is to embrace and accept it. Try to put yourself in their shoes. Whatever feeling they express they are SHARING with you. You need to feel honored that you are trusted enough for them to show you their inner self. If you do, you will be amazed to see the strength of the bond that grows between you. Then with that trusting relationship in place, you will be in a much stronger position to help your child control the negative feelings they experience as normal human beings all do.

This solution worked because I did not apologize or defend myself. I did not say: "Oh sorry, I did not notice you," or "I was busy, I was getting around to it," but instead I acknowledged what the child was feeling. Many teachers or parents try to dismiss the other person's feelings by defending themselves, because they don't like the experience of having someone angry at them. They can't tolerate it so they apologize or defend. Allowing the other person to have their negative feelings, and asking them to explain to you why they feel that way, is supportive and helpful to a child. Expressing feelings does not make you more angry, it makes you less angry, because you connect with someone and share the anger in a non-confrontational way, and that is a healing thing.

Teachers facing their feelings

The examples we have seen so far, show how teachers need to understand a child's feelings, and in order to do that they need to realize that their own feelings are part of the picture. It's as if we see the world through tinted glasses. Whatever a child does is seen by the teacher through his or her own feelings, and is colored by his or her own experiences.

Snapping at the children

When I started teaching I was very puzzled and annoyed at myself because of how the end of the year went. I taught Fifth Grade, and during the year I became very close to the children and they to me. However, at the end of the year, things did not go well. On the last day of school I had a huge task to do, which involved totaling the roll books. It was laborious and particularly annoying for me because (big confession here) I hated math.

I would add across the columns of attendance for every day and week and month, making a total on each page. Then I would total those totals, and the horizontal total was supposed to correspond to the vertical total at the end of the procedure. Of course it didn't. It was an even more difficult task since we were expected to do it in the classroom, on the last day. We were supposed to give the children some work to do, something to write, or draw, or read, while we worked on the roll books.

I would put my head down, start adding. The children would be quiet at first, and then the noise would grow, starting out with a few whispers, it would build and build and I would make mistake after mistake, erasing and redoing it, until the noise was raucous. And then I would start snapping: "Quiet!" That would work for a while, then the noise would build again gradually to another loud cacophony. I would get more and more aggravated, and I would start saying mean things: "I'm so disappointed in you!" I would pick out particular individuals for censure: "You, of all people! You should know better! Don't any of you care that I am working here!" I would be on the brink of angry tears at this point all the while wrestling with the ugly numbers that just would not cooperate with me.

It was only much later that it hit me. I was feeling sad and angry and didn't even know it. I was going to lose this group of children I had grown so close to, and I couldn't think about the sad lonely feeling, so it transformed into helpless anger. Probably anger was an easier feeling to express than sadness. I could not show those feelings at that point in my life, and even now in a classroom setting I would find it difficult to express sadness and loss. I could never bear to say: "I am so sad you are all leaving and we will never have this time back, I've grown so close to you all."

I was probably hiding tears and afraid to cry, and I was not even aware that this is what I was feeling. And so I masked it with irritation. 'Fine! I don't care about the lot of you!' I seemed to be telling myself to cover up my feeling of being left behind. Probably they were feeling sad too, I realized later, and they covered it up by their restless behavior. But that was not clear to me at the time, in fact it did not hit me for many years that this is what was going on.

Teachers NEED an outlet for their feelings. They need to be able to confide in others all the feelings they experience from day to day when dealing with children. This is particularly important for teachers more than other workers, since childhood behaviors can remind us of our own childhood and it is a truly emotional job. A teacher may feel sad seeing a child separating from his mother, or not standing up for himself, or being affected by another child's rejection and that can arouse deep emotions in him from his own childhood.

Staff Meetings – a place to share negative emotions

Teachers need to be self-aware. Part of this self-awareness means knowing when you are experiencing negative emotions in reaction to a child's behavior. If you don't know you are feeling a certain way, chances are you may react unconsciously or 'act out' your feelings. You will be like the driver whose windshield is fogged up, you won't be reacting to what is happening outside you, because you can't see properly.

Bruno Bettelheim speaks in his book *The Empty Fortress* about the importance of understanding ourselves before we can begin to understand others:

> *If we wish to understand the human being in all his intricacy, we must fall back on the earliest method for comprehending man: to know oneself so that one may also know the other. This is why a deficiency in self-knowledge means a deficiency in knowing the other....the introspecting person must also observe and have others observe. Otherwise he cannot verify as being generally true what, for all he knows, may be only his private uncorrected bias."*[17]

What this means for those who nurture children, is that there is an interaction of adult and teacher, observer and observed. You must, as a teacher, as a parent, observe behavior, understand your OWN reaction to that behavior, then take the time to share and verify that observation with others. In staff meetings for instance, teachers can ask other teachers: 'Am I correct in observing that Sheila is often the last one to join in the group?' She may get verification of her observation from the other teachers. "Yes, we have observed that pattern of behavior also, you are not imagining things."

She must then ask herself: 'How do I feel about that?' Does it worry me because I was always shy? Does it annoy me because I was always well-behaved and did what I was told immediately and why can't Sheila do the same? Does it make me frustrated because I don't know how to help her to move into the group? Knowing the self is of paramount importance for teachers and parents. If you don't, the chances are that you will react based on your own feelings, which may not be a helpful or appropriate reaction to the child. You can teach others best when you fully know yourself.

In our school, we bring negative feelings to the table for our staff meetings. One of our weekly staff meetings might go like this:

That parent made me so upset!

> *ME: Let's all think of something that bothered you teachers this week. Something a child, or a parent, said or did that gave you a negative feeling, it can be anything – frustration, anger, fear, sadness, despair. Take a minute and write that down.*
> *Then we will talk.*

> *Then we go around the circle and listen to teachers express a negative feeling.*

> *JOAN: I felt annoyed at Barbara yesterday. She keeps asking me to put her shoes on and I KNOW she can do it herself, she's three years old and I've seen her do it when she thinks no one is looking. I feel so frustrated and angry with her and I don't think I should keep helping her, but then I feel guilty if I walk away. Sometimes I just decide to walk away so I don't show her I feel angry, and to calm myself down.*

> *FRANK: I felt annoyed at Mrs. Belton this morning. She approached me, looking really mad, and asked me where I put Mary's new socks because they were nowhere to be found. I didn't know what to say to her – I told her I'd try to find them, but I felt that she didn't have to speak to me so sharply, she could have said it a different way. I don't even want to look at her next time she comes in.*

> *Then we go around the group asking other people for comments.*

> *TEACHER 1: Yes I get annoyed at Barbara too, she does that a lot, she seems so helpless when she cries about her shoes and that makes me feel helpless too*

TEACHER 2: *I think Barbara is looking for attention, maybe she just needs someone to put her shoes on so she gets attention from us*

TEACHER 3: *That's true – there is a new baby in the family, she might feel jealous because her mother is giving attention to the baby, maybe if she behaves like a baby she will get attention*

ME: *That's true that might be why Barbara acts that way, but we are here to talk about how we feel, so why did that annoy you so much, Joan?*

JOAN: *You know I was the oldest in the family, I never had anyone help me put my shoes on, I had to do it all myself. Maybe it bothers me because of that. I had to be tough and independent, because there was no time for me to be a baby.*

ME: *That's a good insight Joan. You felt that Barbara was looking for attention that you never got, so you felt resentful that you could never demand attention the way she is demanding attention.*

TEACHER 4: *Mrs. Belton can be very assertive, she did the same thing to me about her daughter's new crocs, asking me over and over to make sure I didn't lose them. I never lose kids shoes! I was annoyed too.*

TEACHER 5: *Yes she seems very controlling. But other times she seems very sad when she's saying good-bye, I even saw her crying one day in the hallway after she'd left the classroom.*

TEACHER 6: *Maybe she wants to keep control over the child's things because she worries about being a good mother?*

TEACHER 7: *Maybe it's hard for her to let go of her daughter and she focuses on the shoes and socks?*

ME: *Those are great suggestions. Yes any of these may be her reasons, but remember we are here to think about our reactions, so why does it bother you when she asks you about the socks, Frank?*

FRANK: *It makes me feel like I'm not doing a good job. Like she is criticizing me, and that makes me feel nervous. I don't like being* *judged. I like to feel that I try to do things right and I don't want people to find fault with me. I do feel self-conscious in front of parents in case they are judging me.*

Why does this work?

These kinds of meeting are extremely helpful. Through them, the teachers come to realize that they are reacting not only because outside events are challenging, but also because of their own feelings, their own history. Also, through these honest discussions, teachers come to realize that parents, as well as children, are behaving a certain way because of their own frustrations, anxieties and insecurities.

Children and their parents are not out to 'get' us. They are motivated by something inside themselves – anxiety, fear of separation, the desire to hold on and keep control, for instance. When we understand that motivation, we can interact in much more meaningful and helpful ways. But we also need to realize as teachers that we have our fears, insecurities, feelings of helplessness, and so on, and we have to be aware of those reactions so we do not project our feelings onto others. People react to situations because we have needs and we have experiences that have shaped us and color our perceptions. It's like having smudged glasses, we need to take off our glasses and clean off the smudges before we can see clearly.

After these staff meetings, teachers often come back to me and tell me that somehow, magically almost, the annoying behaviors of children suddenly changed, that very day! Do they really change, or do they change because WE are different, our reactions are now under our control? Self-awareness. That's the real magic!

Teacher accepting negative feelings in self

Stuck at the Park

Angelina is 2 years old. She has an older brother who is 4. It is 8:30 a.m, and Angelina arrives together at school with mom and brother. Her brother runs up the stairs to his classroom, excited to show his friends the new airplane he got. But Angelina takes her time coming in through the front door, her feet are literally dragging on the floor. Her mother is clearly in a hurry as she is also a teacher and needs to be at her job on time. Angelina seems to sense her mother's tension. She stops dead right inside the doorway and says nothing while her mother says in as sweet a voice as she can muster in spite of her frustration:

"Come on, let's go Angelina. Let's go into your classroom, look the teacher is waiting for you!" Angelina won't go into her classroom. She stands in the same place, saying nothing. It is hard to say what she is thinking, as she does not look sad or angry, her face shows no reaction. Angelina loves school, she is happy there, but mornings at drop off seem to fall into the same pattern. This appears to be a time for her to resist whatever her mother wants her to do. Her mother tries very hard not to be upset, she smiles bravely and comes up with lots of tricks to get Angelina into the class, each day a different tactic.

Sometimes the tricks work – one time a game works, another time it helps by being strict, sometimes a bribe of some kind will get her into the classroom. But Angelina seems to learn from each new trick and seems to like to say no to her mother and slow everything down. Her mother breathes deeply and smiles at me, as I am there watching the children arrive. Angelina's mom has discussed this morning ritual and I know how difficult it is for her to keep her cool, not get angry, get her children to school and get to work. I smile supportively, but I know that I should not intervene at this point. Even if I could think of a solution, my advice would help no one and would make Angelina's mother feel even more stressed and inadequate. So I just let the scene unfold. I know that we can talk at another time and I can help her by just listening.

Somehow Angelina's mother finds a way around the resistance and now Angelina is in the classroom, playing happily. It's time for mother to go, and she gives Angelina a hug and a kiss and the door closes and the day is off to a great start. The day goes well for Angelina. For now. Angelina is happy playing with toys, enjoying story time, eating snack. At dance time she lights up, dancing enthusiastically to the music and smiling. And then it's time to go to the park. Everyone gets ready – coats and outside shoes on, and off they go. Hand in hand to the park that's only half a block away.

Running, chasing each other, going on the slides, it's a lovely fall day and the children are enjoying being two years old, being together or playing alone in the sand. Now it's time to leave. And that's when the trouble starts! Angelina won't leave. She sits down on the ground. The Head Teacher cajoles:

"Come on Angelina, it's time to go back to school, we're all ready to leave. Please stand up and hold my hand." The teacher reaches over to her but she folds her arms and turns her back. "We're going to leave, we have to go!" she repeats. There is pressure on the teachers because at 11:30 they have the art teacher coming to the classroom to do a new project with them. The whole group of children and teachers stand and wait to see if Angelina will change her mind, but she won't move. So the Head Teacher turns to Valerie the assistant teacher and says:

"Can you please focus on Angelina, and we will head off now and walk slowly towards the school. We have two teachers so that will be fine. You can catch up with us. See what you can do because we need to get back right now." The rest of the class leaves and Valerie is alone with Angelina. Valerie is feeling a lot of pressure, because now she is on the spot, but she takes on the task. She kneels down beside Angelina and says:

"Angelina, you know the Art Teacher is coming to do some painting with us, she will be waiting for us, can you please come along now so we can get back to school on time?" No luck. Angelina averts her face. Valerie feels frustrated and anxious.

"Well you know, I am going to have to pick you up and carry you back to school if you don't come," she says. Nothing. So Valerie bends down and picks up Angelina. Angelina goes boneless. If you haven't picked up a boneless child then you don't understand how the laws of emotional physics work – a boneless child weighs ten times what a normal child weighs. Valerie sets her down again.

Out of the corner of her eye Valerie sees other parents in the park with their young babies. She assumes these parents are judging her. Valerie starts imagining what they are thinking. They may want to send their child to school soon, and they might be wondering what kind of school this is, what kind of teacher doesn't know how to handle a 2-year old. Maybe the parents are wondering why she isn't being more strict. Maybe they are thinking she is too strict. She feels a lot of pressure is on her to resolve this situation fast, especially with the audience judging her.

And besides that, she thinks that the Head Teacher is probably wondering why she can't get Angelina out of the park and back to school. Her head is full of this pressure and she feels helpless now herself and that makes her feel angry. So she comes up with an idea that is born of desperation. Anything to get the conflict resolved. She will threaten to leave Angelina in the park, she thinks that might work. She's seen other people do it and it worked.

THE SOLUTION

Here is what actually happened...Valerie did indeed lose her cool. "I'm leaving now," she says. She walks towards the gate and does not look back. As she approaches the gate she turns and glances back. But Angelina isn't even looking to see what she is doing. She's still sitting down with her head turned away. Valerie realizes that her game did not work. It appears that Angelina is a better game player and she won. This happens a lot when adults decide to play games to manipulate children into cooperating.

Now Valerie starts to feel panicked. Naturally she can't leave the park without the child, and there is no way she can force the child to leave. She has to face the problem and think about what is possible. In that moment, as always happens when we are calm and go inside ourselves for a solution, one came up. Valerie sat down on the bench beside Angelina and decided that she would be honest. She talks to herself out loud:

"Oh dear, I feel frustrated now," she says. "I don't know what to do. Angelina won't go back to school, and I am worried and can't think – i'm not sure, what I should do?" Now Angelina becomes interested, as children often are when they hear something truthful. She turns to look at Valerie, who notices her out of the corner of her eyes.

Valerie continues: "I am worried that we will miss the art class, and then it will be my fault. I am worried that the art teacher will be mad at me for being late, and not bringing Angelina back in time. But Angelina is not ready to leave, so I just don't know what I can do."

She puts her head in her hands in a pretty real gesture of frustration, with a little drama added for effect. "Gosh, what should I do now?" Now Angelina is intrigued. Drawn into the problem. She thinks maybe she could help. She sees that the teacher is stressed, and she has a solution.

"We could go back now," she says. "I'm ready." In one moment the clouds part and the sun comes out! They walk hand in hand back to school. Later on, after Angelina has eaten lunch and Valerie sits by her at nap time, they have a talk.

"We had a rough time today at the park but we figured it out, didn't we?" Angelina nods. "Angelina, I notice you fight with your mom in the mornings," she says. "You hang back at the door and you won't come into the classroom. I think I might know what's going on. Do you want to hear what I think?"

Angelina nods again. "Is that because your brother always races to get there first and that makes you mad?" Angelina nods once more, glad that the teacher is talking about what bothers her. Whether the teacher is right or not, it is good for Angelina to hear that the teacher is trying to figure out why she is having conflicts with her mom and the teachers. Valerie has realized that Angelina feels small and less important than her brother at times, and she wants to take control and show the world that she has some power – hence her morning struggles and the struggle at the park.

Why it worked

This solution worked because the teacher was able to understand her own reaction to the situation. Once she realized that she felt helpless, that she felt angry because of that helplessness, she was no longer trapped in a frustrated feeling, she was free to think up a creative solution.

Secondly, she was honest with the child – she showed that she was puzzled, at a loss, confused. The child identified with that feeling, since she herself felt that way. In this way the two bonded. All because the teacher permitted herself to accept her own negative feelings and not feel guilty that she was not 'perfect' and calm. Teachers need to be allowed to feel whatever they feel, if they understand their feelings they will not act them out.

Angelina felt small and helpless, and she elicited the same feeling in the teacher. By expressing her own feeling of helplessness Valerie created a situation where the child could come up with the solution. In this way Angelina could save face, gain a sense of control, and yet cooperate with the teacher.

Understanding and accepting family dynamics

Children exist as part of a family. Their behavior is often a reaction to things that might be going on in their lives – a new baby, a mother with health issues, a death in the family, separation and divorce, a move, economic pressures, and so on. Schools must be open to understanding family dynamics and welcoming parents. The more a teacher knows about a family situation the more he or she can understand the child. A teacher should encourage parents to share their problems, so that the school can be a support system and school and parents can work together for the good of the child.

The Hit and Run

James is 2 and he comes to school late a lot of the time. His mother Vanessa has 3 boys, ages 2, 3 and 4, all in school. She is basically operating as a single mother, and she has a high-powered job. Her husband has moved to another country with his new younger girlfriend, and he does nothing to help her parent, so Vanessa has all three children in day care, which puts a strain on her time, her energy, and her finances, despite her high-powered job. She has to travel frequently for her work, and the children are all in school all day, every day. In addition, she often has to have a babysitter pick them up and take care of them in the evenings when she is away, as well as many times on weekends.

When James arrives in school one morning, his mother is rushing and clearly stressed, as she has to drop all three children in different classes. She has trouble being on time because she is tired from having flown back to the city late from a business meeting the night before, and has to make 3 breakfasts and 3 lunches, and get 3 children dressed and ready for school with no help, before going to work herself. This morning she drops James off and he cries for her to stay, but she can't, she has to run and she hugs him then hands him off to the teacher, still crying.

At recess, the Twos class is playing in the backyard. James is having a hard time, grabbing toys, not listening to teachers, running up and down and bumping into other children, he has been behaving like this all morning. James tries to grab a toy shovel from another child, but the child won't let go. James pulls harder. The boy pulls it back. James swings his hand back and slaps the boy hard on the face. Jackie, the teacher, who is nearby, shouts 'No!' but James runs off into the corner and curls up into a ball. The other boy is crying.

Jackie, the teacher closest to James at the moment, feels a rush of anger.

"Why did James have to do that?" she thinks. "He's been causing a lot of problems today. His behavior is escalating into aggression, he can't keep doing this. I'm the teacher and I am in charge, that is a teacher's job to maintain order. I must be strict with James and let him know in no uncertain terms that he did a bad thing, I have to stop him from doing this again so he won't hurt anyone." One of the other teachers is taking care of the boy who is crying, and Jackie goes towards James.

But as she walks towards James who is curled up in the corner, she breathes slowly and processes her feelings. She asks herself what is going on inside herself, and she realizes that she is feeling a helpless kind of anger, and she knows that doesn't feel good for her, and it doesn't help solve problems.

THE SOLUTION

As she approaches James, she starts to ask herself what the child might be feeling. The answer comes to her just from looking at his body language: He feels ashamed. He knows he did something wrong. She asks herself:

"Will it really help if I reprimand him?" She gives herself permission to let go of the 'old way' of reprimand and punishment and searches

inside herself for the right thing to do. She trusts her own instincts and moves closer.

*Jackie bends down so she is on the same level as James. She says "James." But he does not look up, his head is between his knees. She puts her arm gently around his shoulder and he suddenly turns and throws himself into her arms, and he bursts into tears.
She says nothing. He says: "Mommy, mommy," through his tears.*

She sits on the ground and holds him on her lap for a while. Then when he is quiet she says slowly, pausing each time until each sentence sinks in, or until she sees him acknowledging her words:

*- You feel bad because you hit that boy.
- It's OK.
- You are having a rough day.
- You wanted that toy so much that you hit him and you didn't know how to stop yourself.
- You have a lot of feelings today.
- You miss your mommy.
- I know you feel bad about what you did.
- I know you will try not to do that again.*

He listens, the teacher can see he is thinking each time she says something.

They stay there for a while and he sits on her lap until he decides he wants to jump up and go back to play. The teacher reports to the teaching group at our next staff meeting that she noticed James was calmer after that. She felt that he was happy that she understood his feelings, and that she did not punish him any more than he was already punishing himself. She felt that all he needed right then was a hug. She tells the teachers about the follow-up to the event:

At lunchtime when children were eating, she started to talk in general terms how sometimes people do things they don't mean to do and they hurt someone, then they feel bad. She tells us that all the children grew quiet – they wanted to hear about how that works, how people can do things they don't mean to do.

*As the children listened, Jackie went on to say that some people
miss their mommy and it makes them feel sad, or even angry.
Soon as she says this, children start to chime in:*

*"I feel sad sometimes…. I miss my mommy…" and so on. She
notices that James is very calm, listening to the other children, and
she feels that he is glad to hear he is not the only one who gets
these feelings.*

Why it worked

This worked because the teacher was able to see past the child's
behavior to his feelings. She was able to remember all she had
observed about the family situation, and connect that to the child's
seemingly unrelated behavior. He was grabbing at something from
another child – not because he wanted the toy, but because he wanted
a connection that he was missing. In later discussions with James'
mother, the teacher is able to share something about the child's
loneliness and together they work out a plan: When she is leaving for a
trip she will spend more time at goodbyes. She will also give him a little
toy to remind him of her that he can hold when she is leaving.

He will write a letter for his mother, with the teacher's help, draw a
picture or make her a bracelet, to reinforce her presence in the room
with him, and to remind him that he will be seeing her at the end
of the day.

The school and the family work together, to help the child through these
difficulties at separation.

REFLECTING

Rather than reacting to a situation, it is more helpful if adults can simply let a child know what is happening from an outside perspective. Being an objective but empathic witness to what is happening, is a very helpful role for an adult to play.

Reflect a child's feelings

Teachers should reflect what they see rather than trying to fix problems. Stating the obvious is extremely helpful to children. While it is obvious to us that two boys who have so much in common are picking on each other, it can be life changing to them to see their problems in an objective light.

Stating the obvious

Adults should make a habit of letting children know what they see in very simple terms, as if they are observers stating what is happening in a documentary. In this way the child begins to see him or herself almost in a play that is unfolding. That gives the child a sense of perspective on what is happening. Here is how that situation might play out:

A simple reflection:

There are two girls sitting quietly at a table playing with Legos. Neither of them is speaking and the teacher knows that they are both new to the class.

> TEACHER: *There's a red wheel, Sandra is putting the red wheel on the side of that block. It looks like it's going to roll with the two wheels on there. Ahh, it's moving now. Susan has a different idea, she is putting a white block on top of a blue block. I see it's hard to make the blue block fit.*

Why would the teacher narrate the events in front of her like that? The reason is that she may be trying to bring some connection between the children, or else she may be there to be supportive, to draw their attention to what they are doing and how she sees them.

Here is what the teacher is trying NOT to say:

- Why don't you play together?

- Let me help you, I will make the blue block fit for you

- Why don't you make a car?

- You should put another blue block on, then you will have a pattern

- What are you trying to do?

- Why not make a house?

- I will show you how to do it

All of those comments would be intrusive. The child needs to have space and time to do what she wants to do, but at times it is helpful for her to have an empathic observer present, just to reflect back to her what she is doing. This adult can enable friendships or help a child solve problems, simply by stating problems. She can be there if the child asks for help, but should not offer the help before it is requested.

Stating the obvious is very helpful in situations of conflict. It keeps the teacher on track to not get involved emotionally in a child's drama.

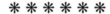

Reflecting conflict to help children work through it

Matt and Jake Fight

Matt and Jake are 3-year-old boys in the same class. Matt's parents have recently separated and Matt divides his time between his father's and mother's apartments. Since the separation, Matt has been easily upset, and more sensitive than usual. Jake's mother is also separating from his father and has a new apartment, soon they will be living apart. Since Jake has found out that his parents are separating, he, too, has been moody and clingy when his mother leaves in the mornings.

It is playtime. Jake and Matt are building with Legos. Things are fine, but suddenly there is a squabble, and Matt is crying. Jake is looking ashamed. I need to step in. I ask: "What's the matter?" Matt says: "Jake hit me," and he is pointing to his lip. It's not bleeding and does not look like a serious hurt, but Matt looks very offended. Jake is looking very emotional, his head is down, he looks ashamed. Now it is decision time. I need to take action.

Here are some ideas that may present themselves to teachers who are well meaning, as good things to do in a situation like this, however they are not good ideas:

- *Tell Jake it is a very bad thing to hit Matt and he must apologize immediately*
- *Ask Jake: 'Why did you do that?'*
- *Ask Jake: 'How would you like it if someone did that to you?*
- *Comfort Matt and try to help him stop crying while glaring at Jake*
- *Tell both boys they must stop fighting*
- *Give Jake a punishment such as time out*
- *Force Jake to apologize*

All of those choices would be short-term solutions that would possibly calm down the situation, temporarily. But they are all designed to make the feelings go away, to bring about a forced apology. At best they are a wasted attempt to solve the children's problems for them. These solutions will not put an end to these kinds of scenes, and they might even exacerbate things, making one child feel like a victim and the other feel like an aggressor.

THE SOLUTION

I decide to do none of these things, as it is not possible to fix problems by imposing punishments. When children are upset it is not the time to force them to think about the other person. It is more important at this stage to listen to the children and have them listen to each other.

*I take the time to pause and reflect, while Matt cries for a little bit,
I lay my arm around his shoulders for comfort. Then I say, not in a
punitive tone, to Jake: 'What's going on with you lately?' Jake throws
his arms around my neck and cries too. At this point I have my arms
around both boys. I wait for a while, as the feelings are coming out
and both boys are crying. Then I ask again: 'Jake, I think you are
having some problems lately, what's happening in your life?'*

Jake is happy to have a chance to say what he is feeling:

*"My dad is going away and he's going to have his own apartment,
my mom is going to have her apartment." I reflect back:
"It's very hard for children when their parents are living in different
places." And I just leave it at that and let it sink in. After a short
while, I have the chance to help to bond the two children.
I turn to Matt and say:*

*"You are going through the same thing Matt, right? Your mom and
dad live in different places now. Is it hard for you living in two
apartments?" Matt nods.*

*Now there is a chance for real listening and connection to happen
between the children: I interpret for them:*

*"See, isn't it strange, you both have the same problems in your lives
right now, and yet you are fighting each other…isn't that weird?"
They look at each other and they burst into laughter. "You can give
each other a hug," I say, and they jump at the chance. "Boys should
help each other if they have the same problem," I say.*

*It is surprisingly quick how the boys forgive and understand each
other. For the rest of the day the two boys are the best of friends.
They are arm-in-arm at story time and not only sit beside each other
at lunchtime, but even share their lunches.*

Why it worked

The technique involved acceptance, and reflection. The children could
not express in words what was bothering them, the teacher needed to
open the doorway to communication for them. This method works on
the principle that first must come acceptance, then reflection, and finally
teaching. You cannot put the cart before the horse. You cannot impose

a solution until the children experience their feelings, and have an outsider reflect what she sees, so they can then see themselves in an objective way.

Once they rise above the situation, and get a bird's eye view of themselves, they can then control their behavior. If you don't know where you are then you can't move towards where you need to go. It's like those maps you look at when you are lost, they have a red dot with the words: YOU ARE HERE. The teacher shows the children where they are. Then they can get to a different place. The teaching in this situation involved explaining to each child that they do have a connection.

Teachers may ask: Where do I get the time for this kind of work? In fact, this particular solution took about five minutes, probably even less. And it was a long-lasting solution as the boys did not engage in fights after that. If I had tried a 'quick fix' with apologies demanded or punishments doled out, the problem would not have gone away, and would probably have worsened.

If the problem was not attended to on a deeper level, undoubtedly it would happen again later in the day. Jake would have felt angry because he was made to feel ashamed. He would have felt misunderstood and more isolated, and the combination of those feelings would have caused more acting out. If Jake were asked why he hit Matt, he would not be aware of the underlying reason. Most adults don't even know why they react in anger, they need time to process their thoughts. How can a child be expected to know why he lashes out? No amount of thinking will help a child especially in the middle of a deep emotion. It is the adult's task to know what the child is going through and to help him to understand himself.

If Jake had been reprimanded, then Matt, 'the victim' would feel like a victim, and helpless. Instead he felt compassion for the other boy, since he saw Jake's tears and heard his life story, and also he felt camaraderie – 'we're both going through divorce situations, we can help each other.' That compassion enabled Jake to feel strong. If I had tried to fix everything, I would have felt exhausted, since it is impossible to force feelings on children. In this case, I felt that I had helped the children develop a real understanding of each other.

I was glad that the children could grow closer, and learn that people should stick together and help each other when they are having

problems. I felt joy when I saw the boys spontaneously bonding. I did not feel the burden of having to be police officer, judge and jury.
I walked home from work, feeling fulfilled and happy knowing I helped in the emotional growth of these two children.

Identifying feelings

Teachers can guide children to identify their feelings even when they are not sure what those feelings are. This can be done in the moment or during an emotional lesson.

Oh dear! I am so embarrassed!

One day I was reading a book to the class titled: "The Monster at the End of This Book."[18] It is a Sesame Street book, and in it Grover talks to the reader and asks the reader to 'please please please don't turn the page'. The reason he does not want them to turn the page is that there is a monster at the end of the book. The tension builds as the teacher turns each page. Grover protests, he says he will lock the book, tie the book in chains, etc. but of course as each page flips over, to the delight and excitement of the children, we get closer to the monster at the end of the book. On the final page, it turns out that the monster is Grover himself, and he says: "Oh dear! I am so embarrassed!"

A little boy called Jason asks me: "What does embarrassed mean?" Suddenly I realize that here is an enormous concept that we all assume children understand, and maybe they do or maybe they don't, but they certainly don't have a word for it. We know what embarrassed means, but do they? And so I try to explain. I find that it is very hard to explain to a young child an abstract concept such as this. I think for a second. I realize that the idea behind the story is that Grover was scared, but then he realizes that he shouldn't be scared, he understands that he had over-reacted. That is a very complex idea, it just won't translate to a young child's ears, so it's time for an impromptu performance. Actions, for young children especially, speak louder than words.

Kelly, the teacher, and I, do a quick whispered rehearsal. We try to come up with a scene that shows a person being embarrassed. We get our story together, and then we put on a show. We put a teddy bear outside the door with its foot sticking inside so the children can see it.

KELLY: *Come on, let's see what's behind this door over here.*

ME: *No, I don't want to, it might be a scary monster!*

KELLY: *I don't think so, let's just see what it is.*

ME: *No no no! I don't want to. It looks like a monster.*

KELLY: *I will go over and see what it is, you just sit here. (She walks over, opens the door, and finds the teddy bear. The children laugh heartily.)*

ME: *Oh, dear, it's just a teddy bear! Why was I so scared? I am so embarrassed.*

KELLY: *You were just scared. I understand. Why are you embarrassed?*

ME: *Because I feel silly, it was just a teddy bear*

KELLY: *But why do you feel embarrassed?*

ME: *Because people are laughing at me.*

KELLY: *Is that what makes you embarrassed?*

ME: *Yes, I don't want people to think I am a baby*

KELLY: *I see. That's what embarrassed means. You don't want people to laugh at you or call you a baby.*

ME: *Yes.*

Why it worked

Children are concrete thinkers. This means they visualize things, they can't think in abstract terms until they are much older. Saying the word embarrassed and defining it in dictionary terms means little to them. Showing them that someone is embarrassed is a more effective way to teach them the meaning of the word. And once you show them, then you can teach them the meaning of the word in depth, breaking apart the layers of meaning to make it relevant to them. After we did this play we did another play where a child does not know the right answer and another child laughs at her and she says: "Now you are laughing at me I feel embarrassed."

Then the other child says she didn't mean to embarrass him. The benefit of this kind of demonstration is to reflect back to the children what their feelings are. It helps them to get their heads around the concepts that they feel but can't quite put a name on. And it gives them an idea how they can respond in certain situations. Referring back to the lesson during daily experiences reinforces the child's understanding of the concept. A teacher can throw the word in there: "Are you feeling embarrassed now?" in an appropriate situation is helpful to cement this notion and attach the word to a feeling.

Being authentic and responsive

It is important to be authentic. What does that mean? It means letting a child know how you feel, but in a non-threatening way. It makes the teacher feel more relaxed being able to be real, and it is also a very natural and effective way of reflecting back to a child how he is coming across to you. Here is an example of how this worked with one girl.

Lucy and Lucinda

Lucinda was a very strong-minded girl. Though she was only 3 years old she seemed very self-assured and independent. She and I had bonded – to a degree – after about a month of her being in my class. She wanted to do things her own way, and I felt she needed to do that, particularly since she had an older brother who was very talented and successful in school, in sports, and so on. I knew she felt competitive with him because at times when she was drawing with other children she would say: 'that's not how you do it, my brother does it this way...'

When I offered to help her with something, she would refuse. She was determined to do it herself. Naturally, I liked that, I admired her can-do attitude and I knew it would help her to be successful in life. However, even though I did not admit it to myself, I felt a little snubbed. When she snapped her coat away from me as I tried to help her put it on, when she said NO! if I offered to pour her glass of water for her, deep down there was a sneaky little feeling I did not allow myself to feel. I felt mad at her for not allowing me to help. Though I did not permit myself to have these feelings, in fact I felt somewhat rejected when she walked away as I tried to offer her a helping hand.

One day something happened to change the nature of our relation ship. From time to time the other children called her Lucy, though her parents called her Lucinda. Some of the teachers called her Lucy at times, and at other times they called her Lucinda, so the names seemed to be interchangeable. And then one day I stepped on a landmine. I sat at the play table and she was passing me by on her way to the bathroom. I said:

"Lucy are you going to wear your boots or your shoes to the park today?" She stopped and glared at me, hands on hips, her eyes blazing.

"My name is Lucinda! Not Lucy!" she said, stamping her foot on the floor. There was a terrible silence around us. In a split second I reacted.

"Okaaay!" I shrugged, using a sing-song voice. Her face was frozen for a second, and then suddenly she burst out laughing. We both laughed. And then she surprised me.

"Do it again!" she said. She wanted us to repeat the scene. So I asked her to walk back and come towards me again, she was to say the same thing and I would say the same thing. We repeated the

scene and laughed again. And so she made me do it over and over, we must have done it ten times. Then I had an idea.

"Why don't we do it the other way around?" I asked. "You be me and I'll be you." We played the game over. This time I said: "My name is Lucinda!" stamping my foot and putting my hands on my hips. She roared with laughter. "Okaaay!" she replied, laughing. I realized that she enjoyed my response. She understood through my gesture that I was annoyed by, yet resigned to her snub. Saying 'Okaaay,' was a way of showing her in a gentle way that her comment was heard and processed, but it left a feeling with me, a feeling of being rejected. I didn't have to labor the point and say: 'you made me feel sad when you said that,' etc. etc. A simple gut response was more connective to her.

Do you know that we played that scene the next day, and the day after that, and the day after that again? She wanted to re-create the interaction between us for weeks on end. Young children often replay things over and over and they do this because they are internalizing the feelings, reliving the event and reinforcing whatever emotional lesson they gained. They are in fact practicing a feeling, a reaction, or a behavior that they like and want to use in the future. They also love role-reversals as they are exploring how other people feel and think, and this helps them put their own actions into perspective.

Even up to the end of the year she would ask for that little play, sometimes we would change the plot, I'd pretend to be going on a trip, I would invite her along, she'd say NO! I'd say 'okaaay!' And we would both laugh. Sometimes she would offer me a treat, I'd say 'no thanks!' she'd say 'okaaay!' She got the general idea of reacting to someone rejecting you, and she was able to play it out in different scenarios.

Why it worked

That interaction with Lucy (sorry, Lucinda!) taught me something. It taught me that children just delight in an honest response. For weeks I had been pretending that her snubs did not bother me. But finally I showed her – in a non-threatening, spur-of-the-moment way, that I felt rejected by her. It wasn't a big heavy conversation – that would never have worked. It wasn't a heart-to-heart chat, which might have appeared to her like a guilt trip. It was a simple reaction that let her know she affected me. I gave her a human reaction. And she appreciated that response.

Playing out that scene over and over again gave her gratification, the gratification of knowing that she did, indeed, have an effect on another person. And that validated her as a human being. Maybe she was shy or defensive, or afraid to be herself before that, but after that time she loosened up and became a fun and popular member of the class. The playing out of a scene over and over is cathartic, I speak about this elsewhere in this book. Catharsis is a way of experiencing a feeling through dramatic play, either watching a play or acting in one. Through replaying a scene, a person can gain mastery or detachment, the initial pain is cleansed and the conflict becomes a story through which a person rises above the situation and sees herself from the outside.

Lucy and I became very close, and she often came to sit together with me in the cozy corner, read a book, or just be quiet together. And I understood it was because I showed her my authentic self. In doing so, she understood that her real self affected my real self. I think the whole interaction made her realize she was powerful, something she had not realized before.

No Forced Apologies

Apologizing is a very misused solution adults use when responding to children's behavior. When a child has done something that is against our social rules, e.g. grabbed a toy from another child, been aggressive or teasing, done something an adult believes is hurtful or wrong, the adult often responds quickly with a "Say you're sorry." Enforced apologies actually create more anger and divide children into victim and aggressor.

Don't get me wrong…apologizing is a very nice social habit. In some cultures it is used very effectively as a convention that diffuses tension and builds connections between people. For instance, in Japan, it's considered very polite to accept responsibility for any slight infraction you may have incurred, even if there is fault on both sides, as a way of showing respect. Say two people bump into each other in the street. It's nice if both of them apologize. After all it is an accident. Even if one of them is slightly more culpable than another, it matters more that both people yield to each other and show they are able to admit they are human.

However, children need to learn to accept responsibility for their feelings. If a child lashes out and hits another child for instance, he may defend himself from retribution by apologizing. The apology seems to make things better by appeasing the angry adult and appeasing the victim. But nothing has changed. The child who has hit will not learn anything except that people get angry at you when you hit. So rather than require an apology, the adult should guide the child towards accepting that there was a reason why he hit the other child.

The goal is to have the child reflect on himself and process the event in an honest way. When he does, the child might realize and be able to verbalize: "I was angry at you because you teased me earlier on today." That insight is far more valuable than the forced apology. It means the child understands the connection between the behavior and the feelings that prompted them. The child accepts responsibility for the action and for his own feelings, and he will probably not repeat this behavior.

It's also very important that children can learn to feel COMFORTABLE with saying they made a mistake, or they were aggressive. If a child can just say 'I was wrong' and feel able to say sorry, quickly and in the moment, that's wonderful. But the wrong way to get to that goal is to enforce apologies. Why? Because it makes the child feel a sense of shame. Let's look at that word and analyze it. What is shame?

SHAME vs GUILT

Guilt is a good thing. If we did not feel bad about doing the wrong thing, we would keep on doing it. Here is an example: I push a door open too quickly and it hits someone who is standing inside. I feel guilty. My action caused someone pain. I did not intend to hurt that person, but I wish I had not hurt them. In that moment I need to make that other person understand that it was not intentional, and I need to make sure they are not hurt.

So I simply say: 'Oh sorry! I opened the door too fast. Are you OK?' If all goes well the other person will say: 'I'm ok. Don't worry.' End of problem. Next time I will try to remember that someone might be standing inside, so I will change my behavior, I will make sure to open the door cautiously. The reason I am more cautious, the reason for changing my behavior, is the bad feeling I had that I hurt someone else. That is the feeling of guilt. In this way guilt is an uncomfortable feeling that helps me to modify my behavior so as not to hurt other people.

A second situation might be where I stole an apple from a fruit stand. In this case I knew it was wrong, and I did it anyway because I told myself it was justified since I wasn't hurting anyone. I figure that they have lots of apples, why can't I take one? Later on I think about this. I see the shopkeeper is going out of business due to high rents. I think about that apple and I feel bad that I took it. If everyone took an apple then that would mean the shopkeeper would go out of business. I realize after the effect, that what I did was wrong.

The guilty feeling stays with me because I have no chance to make amends, it's too late to say I'm sorry. It is not a nice feeling. But it stops me from doing anything like that again. I need to be able to embrace the feeling, understand that I shouldn't beat myself up about it, but just learn from it.

That's guilt, and it's a good feeling to have, we need to tolerate it and know it is helping us to be better people, but not allow it to drown us in negative thoughts about ourselves. However, another, similar feeling is shame, and that is not a good feeling, and it is not healthy or productive, and only leads to negative actions.

Shame is when I feel that I am not a part of the group because of something that I did that was wrong. Shame does not help me to understand other people's feelings, nor does it help me to go back and make amends. It effectively cuts me off from the group, and that compounds the problem, makes me feel unsupported and more likely to have negative feelings to groups of people.

Shame can actually make people do more bad things precisely because they have developed negative feelings towards the group.

Shaming Children

When adults force children to apologize they often do this by shaming them, they may say things like:

- We don't do things like that in our family/classroom

- That's not the kind of thing big boys do

- What's the matter with you?

- I can't believe you could do something like that

- I'm ashamed of you

- Go away from me I don't want to look at you

- What would your parents think of you?

- You hurt that nice girl, how could you do that?

- How could you think of doing something like that?

These kinds of comments create shame. They make a child feel he is not the same as others, that doing bad things is unique to him. These comments can make him feel separate from a group he cherishes. He may begin to believe that something is wrong with him instead of accepting that he had negative feelings like everyone else does and forgiving himself for his weaknesses.

Children find it very hard to apologize when they are shamed. They feel so bad about themselves that they just can't connect with the other person. An apology should be very lightly suggested and not enforced. If an adult wants to help a child to say sorry he could help and guide the child to understand why they did what they did, and afterwards suggest non-humiliating ways of making amends, like bringing some ice to heal a wound, or a tissue for tears.

When the situation is cooled down afterwards, the adult can talk to the child about what it was that made him do what he did. 'I think you probably felt jealous, that's why you did that,' for instance. Forcing apologies will not help in a situation where a child feels ashamed.

However, children should be encouraged to say sorry quickly and easily if they step on someone's toes, or do something accidental. They need to just say sorry quickly and easily so they get to realize how quickly other children will forgive them, and apologizing becomes a routine courtesy that does not involve shame.

Building group understanding through reflecting on conflicts

We win, you lose!

It's 10:15 a.m. The group of four-year-olds are done with free play and now are sitting in a circle in front of the teacher. She reads a story to them. The teacher is aware that the children love the story, they are all very involved, and paying attention. But she also notices that the children have situated themselves so they are sitting next to the person they most like, as usual. She is aware that at age 4, being with the friend you like is probably the most important thing in your day, and this can be more important than what is going on in class. What other people think of you may be to some children the most important part of their day in school. Story ends. The teacher looks around at the children and says:

"After snack is outside play. We could go to the park today. Or we could go to the backyard and play with our new water table. What do you think?" There is a loud clamor.

"Backyard! Park!" The teacher is used to this kind of situation and she knows in advance what she will do.

"You are all shouting so I can't hear your answers," she says. "But I can see that some people want park, some people want backyard, so what do you think we should do?" The children know what they usually do in this situation: "VOTE!" They call in unison. The teacher has helped them to understand that this is a process they can use when they can't agree.

Though she makes a lot of the decisions about the classroom, the teacher wants to allow the children to have a say in their day. She

97

realizes that conflict is a part of life, and it is important to teach children that there are various ways of dealing with conflicts. One of those ways is to vote. And so she begins the voting process. She takes her marker and draws two pictures on the chart beside her chair, one of a water table which donates the backyard, and one of a slide, denoting the park. She draws a line down the middle.

She goes around the circle of children, asking what each child wants to vote for, one by one. 'Park' the first child, a popular young boy called John, says. Sitting next to him is his best friend, Jamal, who of course, to be the same as his best friend, says "Park" and smiles, checking John's reaction to see how John will approve of him because he's voted for the same thing. The teacher marks one vote, then another, under the drawing for Park. John and Jamal are both delighted. They have each voted for the same thing, and that makes them feel happy since they are friends, and now they are made closer by voting for the same thing, and they also feel they have helped one other by voting for the Park. They applaud each other by smiling, slapping each other on the back.

As the teacher goes around the room, she notices that one by one, the children all seem to vote for the park, and each time a child votes for park, the teacher makes a mark on the chart. The children are delighted. They clap and laugh each time a mark goes into the column they have selected. The teacher is starting to feel uneasy. She is wondering if one by one the children are just deciding to be part of the group rather than stating what they really want. She knows this can happen a lot at this age. Are they feeling peer pressure? But she respects their decision and keeps marking the votes in the column to which they belong.

And now everyone has voted except for the last boy, Phoenix. He is a quiet boy, shy, usually on the outside of the group, and to the teacher it appears at times that he may have a hard time joining into a group that is already formed. The teacher has tried during the year to get him to be assertive, with some degree of success. And now everyone has voted but him, and the teacher turns and looks at him.

"Phoenix, backyard or park?" The children can't even keep still in their spots, they are ready to give a big cheer, the excitement is tangible. Phoenix thinks for a second and he says: "Backyard."

The teacher makes a mark under his name, it is the only vote for the backyard. Then she asks which side has more votes and they all call out "Park!" Phoenix looks sad. John yells out and points at Phoenix:

"We win, you lose!" and then Jamal says it too and they chant a couple of times "We win, you lose," and there is some laughter from the children, followed by an uneasy silence. The teacher gets a sudden rush of indignation, but she tries to not react with a sharp reprimand to John and Jamal but instead to give herself a few seconds to think about what is the right response.

She realizes that she has a lot of feelings and she is aware that it is best to wait and let her own feelings die down before she reacts.

THE SOLUTION

The teacher is aware of some of her feelings. She remembers that when she was little she was very shy and had a hard time making friends. Phoenix reminds her a lot of herself, and at this moment she is tempted to yell at John and Jamal and tell them they should not say hurtful things. She thinks maybe she should protect Phoenix and tell him not to worry, and to say to the other boys that this is not nice behavior.

But she knows that this might actually turn the children against each other, making Phoenix into a victim and the boys into aggressors. She also knows that John and Jamal need to understand their own actions and process the consequences without being punished. Her job is to help everyone come to an understanding of what just happened, to help Phoenix to express himself, and to help him to make meaningful connections with the other children. And also to help the two boys understand their own behavior. So she turns to Phoenix and says:

"Phoenix, you are the only boy who voted for the backyard. I notice that John and Jamal said 'We win, you lose!' I would like to know how you feel about what they just said." Phoenix puts his head down.

"I didn't like it," he says.

The teacher says: "I want you to tell them that, please look directly at them and tell them how you feel about what they just said."
The whole group is listening now, even more intently than they did to the story. Generally Phoenix does not say much, but this time Phoenix looks over at his friends.

"I didn't like it when you said 'We win you lose,'" he says.

"Phoenix, please tell them why you didn't like that," the teacher says.

"I wanted to go to the backyard, so I want to be a winner too," he says. The teacher turns to John and Jamal.

"Do you see how it makes Phoenix feel when you say that?" she asks. She is not using a harsh tone, she is simply asking a question, in a very neutral tone. They nod. They look like they are realizing something they had not thought about.

"What do you think he feels?" The children are squirming, they feel guilty. "Anyone know what the word is?" she asks, eager to make sure they are thinking of this in a logical almost scientific way. This takes the guilt out of the situation.

"I think he feels bad," one boy says.

"Yes, that is right he is feeling bad, but what's the exact word for what he feeling, is he feeling sad, angry, left out..." she prompts.

"Left out," is the general consensus. The teacher moves on quickly. Her goal is not to make anyone feel responsible for someone else's feelings, just to convey the idea that in a group, different people feel different things. And to illustrate the fact that it's important to put a name on our feelings. She continues:

"As a matter of fact, I think Phoenix is a real winner today, do any of you know why?" There is a silence. The children do not have an answer. They are grasping to think what the teacher will say. She tells them:

"I think Phoenix is a winner because he picked something he wanted even when everyone else wanted something different. Sometimes we are afraid to say what we want when we know everyone else disagrees with us. Do you notice that we sometimes do things just so we can have our friends like us?" The children nod. "It takes a lot of courage to say something that is different, when your friends all want you to say the same thing that they think."

She turns back to Phoenix and asks him: "Are you disappointed that you did not get what you wanted?" He nods. She smiles. "I know you are disappointed, and we have to do what the group voted for, but I am proud of you that you said what you wanted, and also that you told your friends how you feel."

The teacher watches as the group gets ready for snack. Out of the corner of her eye she notices John and Jamal approach Phoenix and put an arm around his shoulder. She overhears John saying: 'Next time you will get your choice.' She is gratified that the children have been thinking about what happened, and have come up with a word of comfort to their friend.

She also feels good that she has seen such growth in Phoenix, he has had the courage to be different. Openly expressing his difference actually helped him find his way into a group of friends rather than complying with the group or compromising his own individuality in order to be popular.

Why it worked

The teacher was able to recollect her own childhood feelings of being left out of a group, and to realize how important those feelings are to children. She knew that she was feeling anxious and angry at the two boys for making Phoenix feel bad. That angry feeling belonged to HER and not to Phoenix, so she gave herself a minute to process that feeling before saying or doing anything. She realized she should let go of her goal to cheer Phoenix up, and any thought of making the other children feel bad.

Her true goal was to have children see that there are other feelings besides their own. And her second goal was to support Phoenix in his decision to go against the group, since he had been afraid to do so before. By asking him to express his feelings rather than interpreting them for him, she gave him power. By asking the other children to imagine what he might be feeling she got them to think about how actions can affect other people.

By validating his disappointed feeling, she allowed Phoenix to process his disappointment in his own way – we don't always get our way and we need to accept that. Phoenix did not get his wish. But he did assert himself – and that growth was for him a much more important milestone.

Feeling a child's feelings

No! I Won't Put on My Boots!

> *It's 10:30 a.m. Time to go out to the park. The three-year olds are done with snack. Some of them are in the bathroom. Some of them are getting their coats and shoes on. Some of them already have their coats and shoes on, and are sitting with books waiting for the group to be ready to go out. There are 15 of them, in various stages of transition to outside time.*
>
> *There are three teachers. One of them is getting the backpack ready for the park with water, Band-aids, ice packs, wipes, and other essentials for a regular school park trip. (Always be prepared!) The second teacher is helping with coats or helping children to LEARN how to put coats on so they can become independent. This teacher is encouraging everyone to stay on track and finish getting their coats and shoes on instead of wandering off and getting distracted with talking to others, or playing with a toy, or generally forgetting what's going on in the 'real' world.*
>
> *The third teacher is cleaning up after snack, making sure the children in the bathroom are not just sitting chatting, reminding them from time to time that everyone is waiting to leave. This is a typical classroom transition scene – the teachers are busy with keeping children on track to go out, while trying hard not to nag or not to rush anyone. This is a challenging task in itself for teachers, to keep a group of 15 children moving towards their goal, while still allowing*

them the time and space to think about what they are doing and making conscious decisions themselves.

The goal is to have the group move in an organized but non-regimented way, because there is nothing more detrimental to a child's good will than being nagged or yelled at, or overly organized. This turns children into passive and compliant 'cogs in a machine' and doesn't help them feel part of the group's mission. Still, they only have an hour in the park, as they have to be back in time for lunch, and today they are having a special visit from one of the parents who is bringing in cupcakes for her son's birthday. So pressure is there for everyone to move in the same direction, with some speed.

Now it's 10:45 a.m. The children in the coats and shoes are getting a little uncomfortable, it's warm in the room. They are done with their reading and anxious to leave. The children in the bathroom are done and working on coats and shoes, and the teachers are shuttling those who are ready towards of the door, while striving to get the 'stragglers' up to speed so teachers can count the children (a necessary routine) and get ready to leave.

Veronica is sitting in the corner. She has her coat on but she is not showing any inclination to move or to put her new pink boots on.

"Come on Veronica, let's go!" the Head Teacher calls. Veronica does not answer. The teacher takes a long look at her. It's clear from her body language that Veronica has no intention of moving. Her head is down, she is turned towards the wall.

"Veronica, you need to get your boots on, we're waiting to go to the park!" the teacher calls again, in a sweet tone that is also firm, she is trying not to get rattled. Still no move. The teachers look at each other.

"Mark, can you go and help her?" the Head Teacher asks Mark, the assistant teacher. She knows that Mark is particularly good with Veronica, who can be moody at times, and does not respond well to nagging or pressurizing. "We will go downstairs and wait for you." The group of children move out to the corridor while Mark goes over to Veronica.

Mark is under some pressure now. The Head Teacher has asked him to help Veronica, but he knows how she can be difficult, and stubborn at times, and he has no idea how he is going to handle this situation, especially since everyone is waiting. There is a time crunch, they have to be back in time today for a the birthday cupcakes, the parents of the birthday boy will be there on time, waiting anxiously to begin the celebration. He feels tense.

"Come on, Veronica," Mark says. "Do you want me to help you on with your nice boots? These are new, right?"

"No!" Veronica says. "I won't put on my boots!" She turns away from him and from the door he can see the head teacher looking at him, clearly wondering how long this is going to take. He feels like yelling COME ON NOW VERONICA, JUST CO-OPERATE CAN'T YOU? But he knows that's not a good idea. So he tries to think for a minute.

THE SOLUTION

Luckily, Mark understands that he will be supported by the Head Teacher and the school management in whatever he does. Even though there is always some pressure to get things done in a certain time frame, Mark knows that the school values his input as a creative individual who can come up with solutions that are not written down in a book of rules. Knowing this, he takes the pressure off and gives himself a minute to gather himself and draw on his inner resources. Mark realizes that he is feeling angry and frustrated. He sees that Veronica is resistant to putting on her boots, so something has got to happen, but he does not know for sure what it is. He decides to try to talk to Veronica.

"Hey, do you like your new boots?" he asks.

"No!" Veronica says.

"Oh, I thought you liked pink. Isn't pink your favorite color? I know yesterday it was." Veronica says nothing.

"You like boots, right?" Veronica nods.

"But not these ones?" She shakes her head.

"Why not?" Veronica starts to cry.

"These are my cousin's boots. They're broken, see?" Veronica points to the buckle at the side which has popped open and needs fixing. "Everyone will laugh at me."

Mark opens his mouth. He is about to say: 'No one is laughing at you. The boots are fine. No one notices that buckle but you. Don't worry you look nice,' when he remembers something from his childhood. Something just like that happened to him.

"I know just how you feel," he says. "Want to hear a story about me when I was little?" The other teachers and children have faded off in his mind. He can hear them going down the stairs, but he has become totally focused on his work with Veronica. He is in a creative place now, remembering something similar that happened in his life. Veronica is not crying any more – she is wide-eyed, and obviously wants to hear about when Mark was a child. She looks at him now with interest and nods. He begins his story.

"When I was little my mother bought me a straw hat and she made me wear it to school. I HATED that hat. One of the other kids called me a girl when I wore it and I just hated wearing it, but my mother made me put it on before I left in the morning because she thought it looked great. I felt just like you do. I didn't want to go to school and have people make fun of me. You want to know what happened to that hat?"

"Yes." Veronica is engrossed.

"I was walking over the bridge one day when the wind blew it off my head, and I watched it as it blew away, and I didn't run after it. That was the end of the hat. It went floating down the river." They both laughed.

"You hated that hat?" Veronica says, delighted to have someone share her feelings.

"Yes. My mother thought it was adorable, but I didn't." Veronica wants to hear the story over again. He tells it again, aware that the class is probably waiting for them downstairs, but realizing that some things take time and are worth doing.

"I know you don't like the boots, but can we just put them on this one time and go to the park? I will tell your mommy to fix the buckle or get you a new pair if she can." Veronica nods. She is happy that Mark has figured out what is wrong. That is more important to her than the boots at this point. Mark is happy that he has taken the time to understand Veronica and that he did not act on his frustration by pressurizing her. They go outside quickly and find the group waiting for them, playing a counting game until they arrive.

Why it worked

The teacher found himself in a stressful place – the head teacher needed him to get the conflict resolved so the whole class could go to the park, but the child was clearly not going to move out of the conflict readily. He had to struggle with that conflict himself first and then accept that the most important thing he could do right there is to work with the child in terms she could relate to. That letting go of the feeling of pressure was the first step in reaching a solution.

Secondly, after he had decided that the child's problem was a priority, he had to think how he could relate to her problem and then have her understand that he did relate. He understood her situation – being forced to wear something you do not like – and that understanding reminded him of a situation that he had been in as a child. That is an example of feeling the child's feelings. If an adult can do that, it is REAL empathy, not just mouthing a fake 'oh well, you are sad' token acknowledgement.

Then, thirdly, after he remembered the story, he presented it to the child in a fun and interesting way. Through the story, she understood that he felt her feelings. Children relate in CONCRETE ways to the world. The teacher could have said: "I understand your feelings. I felt the same way one time." But that is not as concrete as a story. With a hat, flying off a bridge into the water. Through the images he presented to her, she knew that he understood her. And being understood is, after all, what everyone needs. No lectures. No advice. No reprimands. 'I understand you' are probably the three most powerful words in the world. And the teacher conveyed that concept to the child in a story.

Feeling someone else's feelings often involves abandoning our own scripts. Sometimes we see a child who is suffering in a certain way and we can't bear that suffering, it reminds us of something in the past, so we try to rush past it instead of engaging in it.

One day I was in the supermarket and a little boy was crying while his mother was paying the cashier. The male cashier, an older man, said to the child:

"Come on now, that's enough, big boys don't cry!" I honestly could not just let that go. I understood that he was trying to help the mother, but I opened my mouth and said:

"You know that's not true. Boys need to cry as much as girls, and they should be allowed to. Crying is good for you, keeping tears inside can be very detrimental to children." The man just looked and smiled thinly, I am not sure what he thought, but I felt that at least I had put out some truth into the situation.

I can only guess that this man had been told that during his childhood and might be carrying some emotional pain that he had never even thought about. He could not feel the little boy's feelings because he had been taught to stifle his own.

TEACHING

Teaching the Family

Every child is part of an original group called the family. Teachers need to apprehend the nature of each family through open discussion with parents or caregivers. Teachers need to greet not only the child but also the family. They need to create an open atmosphere and a willingness to listen and understand anything the family is prepared to share.

Every family is different and every family goes through its own emotional struggles, changes and adaptations to the circumstances that it meets. Teachers need to keep abreast of the family's struggles in order to provide a supportive network for them and their child. This can be done at parent meetings, and in brief interactions at pickup and drop off.

Since most of us have not been emotionally educated, and most parents struggle with their child's raw emotions, it is important for the school to provide guidance to the parents. Teachers can create blogs, write newsletters, send emails to parents, and help them understand what is going on in their child's psyche. Parent workshops are also a great place for parents to gain support from other parents and supportive school staff.

Here is a blog, which I wrote to help parents understand how to handle a child's innocent and sometimes embarrassing expressions.

CENSORSHIP OF CHILDREN

I hate you mom!

What is censorship? It is the act of supervising the words – or actions – of the self and others, and the prohibiting of words or actions that may be deemed dangerous to the well being of the group. This is a contentious issue, particularly in the realm of politics, sexuality, race, and religion, and as we have seen lately these subjects can be extremely difficult to navigate.

However in this case I would like to refer to the topic of censorship of children. Children, as we know, begin their life with no awareness of the needs of others. In addition they have not learned the full range of words, tones, inflections, and the many subtleties of human communication. In order to be heard and have their needs met, babies have to scream and cry. They do not yet understand that there are other ways to get what they need. That comes with time. Words are the key to communication, but young children do not instinctively understand the power of their own words, or the ways in which words can be modified or balanced with other words or inflections of the voice to different effect. They often go from zero to a hundred in order to get the attention they feel they need.

For instance, a three-year-old child might feel angry at a perceived slight and her response might be: 'I will never invite you to my birth day party ever again'. Or a little boy might have picked up some words that seem powerful because they produce a reaction, and instead of saying 'I'm angry' he will lash out with 'you're stupid.' Perhaps he is angry with his parent and he says: 'I hate you.'

A child on the bus might see an overweight person and say: 'Look at him he's SO FAT!' or in a cafe she might see a man with big ears and a small nose and say 'Look at the MOUSE guy!' or in the elevator a large woman wearing a lot of makeup and a brightly colored dress enters and the child says: 'Hey look it's a CLOWN!' (these are all real incidents).

What is a parent or teacher to do? A first instinct might be immediate and unconditional censorship:

- How dare you say you hate me!

- Never say that word again in this house.

- Stupid is not a word we use.

- You are forbidden to say that.

- Never call anyone fat. It's not nice. How could you?

That kind of response works for a short-term solution. It scares the child, serves as a prohibition. The child realizes she can't say words *such as hate or stupid or fat, though she doesn't know why. But how does that help a child? What censorship of words does is teach a child that there are a set of powerful words that cannot be used, even though she does not understand them. Is that a good life lesson? The parent is attempting to control the child, and of course that is a good impulse, children do need to learn to control what comes out of their mouths just as they need to control their behavior. But is controlling the child's words by censoring the actual words the best way to teach a life lesson?*

What a parent or teacher should be aiming to do is to get at the root issue, and to teach the child the core values of society. The core value of any society or any group, even if it's a group of two people, should be that each person is equal in value, and each person should be listened to with respect and talked to with respect. People should communicate their feelings openly and honestly and take responsibility for their own feeling, rather than blaming, threatening or scapegoating others with names. That's what we need to teach.

So is it disrespectful for a child to say to a parent 'I hate you?' The answer is no. A child's statement 'I hate you' is her unskilled and uneducated way of saying: 'I feel anger.' And a child's statement: 'I'll never invite you to my party,' is his way of saying 'I feel hurt by what you just did.'

When a child says to you: 'I hate you,' or 'You're stupid,' instead of saying 'Stop, don't say that!' a better response would be: 'I hear you are angry. Tell me what is making you angry.' And AFTER you have listened to your child's feelings, you can teach the child that in future he or she should say: 'I am angry' instead of calling names, threatening, or using 'hot' words like 'stupid.' You can explain that calling names is a bad thing because that just passes the anger on to the other person, rather than building bridges between people.

As for the incidents on the bus and the elevator, it's important for us to remember that a child sees the world in very brightly colored ways. To a child, new things are startling, cartoonish, dramatic, and highly stimulating, and they are just innocently stating what they see, their intention is not to hurt feelings. If you can, try not to react in the moment out of embarrassment but later explain that some people will be hurt if they are called fat, and that it's best not to comment on how someone looks because we value how others feel and our words are powerful, and can hurt.

Censorship is a band-aid. Though we do need to censor our selves in many situations, it would be a more peaceful world if we could say what we feel in a non-aggressive way, and take responsibility for our own feelings, instead of lashing out, calling names, or threatening to banish the other person who has aroused those feelings. We all feel angry, scared, rejected at times, and it's important to recognize and share those feelings and not act on them or shove them out of sight by censoring them.

Putting on 'shows' to illustrate emotional situations

Children learn best from examples so this is an illustration of how we created a lesson by acting out a situation that caused us problems in the class.

The Constant Interrupter

We had a recurring situation in our class that made us a little uncomfortable, and none of the teachers were sure of the best way to handle it. A teacher would start reading and it would go like this:

Teacher: *"Today we're going to read this book about dinosaurs...."*

Jim: *"Oh..oh...oh...I went to the museum and I saw dinosaurs and they were..."*

Teacher: *"That's interesting, John. We'll talk about that in a little while. Let's start reading, though, as everyone seems to want to hear what's in the book. Now this dinosaur here is a T-Rex...."*

Jim: *Oh..oh..oh...I saw a T-Rex when I went to the museum....*

Mary: *Stop!! You have to stop talking when the teacher is reading.*

Jim: "But I saw the T-Rex, it was big...it was...

Teacher: "That's so exciting Jim, but now let me just go ahead and read the book. Anyway, a long time ago these dinosaurs walked the earth. Here's a picture of a T-Rex attacking another dinosaur...

Jim: Oh..oh..oh..he's eating him. There's blood on him...

Mary: No! Don't talk!! We can't talk!!

Jim: Aaahhh I want to tell you...

Teacher: Now that's enough now. Everyone be quiet. I am going to finish the book and then we can all get a turn to talk.

This situation was happening quite a lot. Jim was so engrossed in whatever story was being read that he could not contain his excitement. The teacher was delighted to see such enthusiasm. She tried to get him to be quiet but his excitement would not be held back, so she would let him say a couple of things since he was so enthusiastic about the story and so involved in it. Yet other children wanted to listen and to follow the rules and they took it on themselves to shush him and that created more distraction in the story, and the teacher had to intervene.

The teachers had a meeting, the three of us sat down and discussed it. We all felt the same conflict, none of us knew where to draw the line. We did not want to dampen Jim's enthusiasm, however we were tired of constantly telling him to wait, and also we were concerned that the other children were anxious to follow the rules and they could see that Jim did not. This didn't seem fair to them. But what to do? We decided that there were a few options:

We could just make a clear cut rule, NO TALKING during a story

We could stop every story we are reading and allow everyone to talk

We could say only excited people can talk during the story

None of those options seemed perfect. Besides, none of us likes setting arbitrary rules because there might be a time when we would welcome an interruption, let's say a child might want to correct something the teacher had missed or mistakenly said, or might have a very good insight that we wanted to welcome into the reading. In general we do not like hard and fast rules as they may preempt creativity BUT we need to respect the group as well as the individual.

THE SOLUTION

We realized that since we were having a tough time thinking of a solution, what we probably should do is present this problem to the children. So we decided to do a performance. We would act out the scene just as it had played out in our class many times, and then we would see what the children had to say.

I was playing the TEACHER and the other two teachers were playing the parts of THE INTERRUPTER and the GOOD GIRL. We introduced this performance to the children by telling them we have a problem in our class and we were going to do a show about it. We began the show. I started reading from a very popular book.

TEACHER: Here is a book about SuperDuperman

INTERRUPTER: I have that book!

TEACHER: Let's go on. I wear a red cape

INTERRUPTER: I have a cape like that one at home!"

GOOD GIRL: "SHHHHHH!!"

TEACHER: I can fly when I wear my red cape.

INTERRUPTER: I can fly too!

GOOD GIRL: SHHHHHH

TEACHER: If anyone is in trouble I can save them.

INTERRUPTER: One time I put on my red cape and...

GOOD GIRL: STOP TALKING!!

TEACHER: What's going on here?

GOOD GIRL: She's talking and I'm trying to listen

INTERRUPTER: But I have a cape...

GOOD GIRL: I can't hear (covers ears)

TEACHER: This is a problem. One person wants to talk about the story. The other one wants to listen. I don't know which one is right and which one is wrong. (I turn to the group of children). We have a problem here. What do you think the teacher should do?

CHILDREN: She should be quiet. She can't talk.

TEACHER: But she's excited, she wants to share her ideas.

CHILDREN: She can talk.

TEACHER: But this other girl wants to hear the story. And she wants to talk, I am not sure which one is right? (Now the children grow very excited and start to call out)

CHILDREN: She can't talk. She can. She can't. She needs to wait. She should take turns. (Everyone is talking at the same time.)

Suddenly a boy shouts out: GRRRRRRR. He puts his hands up like claws and says: I'm a dinosaur. Munch...munch....

TEACHER: Why are you growling?

GROWLING BOY: I'm going to eat her. Because she's not listening.

TEACHER: I think you're mad at her because she's not listening. Well she is listening actually, but you're mad at her because she's interrupting? Suddenly a girl jumps up and runs in front of the two 'children' who were having the problem.

GIRL: *This one over here is quiet and this one is not quiet! You can't talk while the story is redden. (sic)*

TEACHER: *(looking at the whole class) You think it's not OK to talk while the teacher is reading the story? Do you all agree?*

CHILDREN: *Yes.*

TEACHER: *So this girl can never ever say anything?*

CHILDREN: *Yes. No. She can talk. She can't say anything.*

TEACHER: *So when can she say anything?*

CHILDREN: *At the END of the story.*

TEACHER: *Oh, so she can talk but she has to wait to the end of the story?*

CHILDREN: *Yes.*

TEACHER: *(I turn to the teacher who plays the interrupter) So you get very excited and you find it hard to wait. Is that right?*

INTERRUPTER: *Yes*

TEACHER: *But can you try to be calm and wait until the end of the story?*

INTERRUPTER: *Yes, I'll try.*

TEACHER: *So that is the end of the story. They all lived happily ever after.*

That was the end of our performance. The children became very involved, wanted to pick sides, wanted to offer solutions, wanted to BE in the story. It took them a while to calm down afterwards, they became so involved! Later, the teachers discussed how well it went. We felt that the children themselves got inside the problem, lived it

so to speak, and came out of it with a solution. We now had a strategy, if there was an interruption we would say "Remember that you should wait to the end of the story. But guess what?
The problem did not happen again, and everyone did live happily ever after!

Why it worked

Drama always works if you want to make a point! Putting on a show is one of the best ways a teacher can illustrate an issue she knows is going on under the surface. However, it must be remembered that putting on a show should not be done to show the 'right' way to behave. Teachers who try to do that will be disappointed. Children are eager to see the conflict, not necessarily the solution.

CATHARSIS

Ask yourself why you go to films about war, or plays about tragic love, why you read books about struggle, disaster, and survival? Writers often refer to the term 'catharsis.' The definition of the Greek word is literally: cleansing. In a literary or psychological sense, the word has come to mean: 'the process of releasing, and thereby providing relief from, strong or repressed emotions.' Aristotle said:

> *"Tragedy is an imitation of an action that is serious, complete, and of a certain magnitude; . . . through pity [eleos] and fear [phobos] effecting the proper purgation [catharsis] of these emotions"*[19]

We like to experience difficult moments through drama and literature and this cleanses us and relieves us of the tension we feel.

Catharsis occurs when a person experiences conflict in a vicarious way through watching a show. We relive our struggles, much like we do at night when we dream. If you watch a child's face when she is at a show you can see the emotions that over take her while she experiences other people enacting a drama. This is what is called catharsis. It is a strange and quite mysterious process in which we are cleansed through viewing a dramatic incident in a movie, play, puppet show, etc. We come away feeling a sense of relief, just because we let ourselves be open to deep feelings, and have them wash through us and cleanse us. It is not the resolution of the problem which brings about the healing, it's the re-experiencing of deep emotions that somehow magically helps us to deal with our own inner conflicts.

In psychoanalysis, catharsis means reliving a painful experience in a safe place. When a person can feel strong enough to remember something that has been kept out of mind due to its painful nature, he or she can feel relief. Often when old feelings that come up can cause a person to cry or express outrage, and this has a healing effect so the person can take a step forward and not be tied on to the old hurt. People who have PTSD very often have had to keep frightful memories out of their minds because their first survival tactic was to just get through the experience. They often do not have the time or the luxury to feel anything. Later on, in a safe place, they may relive the traumatic incident and this helps them to have catharsis, a relief, a feeling of being released of a burden, a cleansing.

In the case of our story of The Interrupter, the drama is a tragedy in which one child wants to be heard and the other child does not want him to interrupt the story. The reason that is a tragedy is that there is a conflict, which causes negative emotions on both sides, and this conflict cannot be reconciled. Two emotions are bouncing around out there, bumping into each other, much as hot air and cold air bump into each other and cause stormy weather. It's a tragedy and not a comedy, because there is no resolution. When the play comes on, the children can see the two sides of the problem played out before them, and that is where the cleansing or catharsis comes in.

If only one side of the situation were to be shown, there would be no drama. But the teachers present a situation where there is no clear answer – both sides feel equally strongly, and both are, in a sense, right. That's where the tension is created in the audience, and through that tension the audience experiences the problem from the outside, as viewers. Children get to see as from above instead from within, and that is instructive.

Putting on a play with a specific area for the show to happen and a place for the audience to sit is an important convention. That is because it helps to relive situations of conflict or struggle in safe settings. The show is out there and we are over here, watching at a distance. It is also helpful to be surrounded by other audience members. Watching the conflicts play out, we can appreciate that conflict is universal, other people feel the same way as us. Knowing everyone goes through the same or worse situations is comforting.

IMPORTANT NOTE ABOUT PERFORMANCES AND YOUNG CHILDREN:

When younger children see their own struggles expressed in dramatic form, they often have a visceral reaction – they are experiencing catharsis and this can generate an intensely physical response in children. It is important to first show them the struggle, and then bring them back into a calm situation, and follow with a discussion. You may find yourself trying to superimpose a 'solution' – your adult self may want to correct the conflict, and show children are all being nice to one another, but you will probably be disappointed if you try to do this. You will find that children do not want to jump straight to a solution – they will beg you to see the struggle again!

They will want to see the conflict over and over again. It's part of their process. When you show them the struggle, you may find they will become highly agitated, as they haven't yet learned that the 'play' and the reality are separate. You are releasing feelings that they have been working hard to keep under control, and that can be intense for them. They may scream out loud with impassioned laughter, that is recognition of something that has been suppressed.

They have not developed self-control to the degree an older child or adult would, so they may want to join in the show, rush onto the 'stage,' BE the characters, roar, start speaking lines as if they are in the play, respond to the actors and tell them what they are doing wrong. They don't know there is an imaginary line that divides the play from the audience.

The second very important stage in this teaching step is to help children to process those feelings and discuss them. Calming can be done in any number of ways that teachers will have access to, singing, counting, moving to a discussion corner, some way of transitioning back from active mode to thinking mode.
This calming down process and reflective analysis should be done after

children have been to see movies or watched TV shows. Children can be very easily aroused into fear or anger through TV watching, shows, etc. Adults should work with them to discuss the feelings they experienced, and as children grow older they should be encouraged to analyze what it was that made them feel that way – what tricks did the actors or the author use to elicit feelings in them.

Training children to communicate clearly

A child is part of a group in school. Every child feels the need to belong. Being part of a group involves conflict. The individual child has his own needs and desires. Teachers need to help children to maintain their individuality and at the same time become part of a group. When children try to communicate they have to overcome obstacles.

There are techniques that adults can help them in order to work through some of these problems that occur when one or two children are trying to get along:

> Bullying
>
> Exclusion
>
> Using a hurtful tone of voice
>
> Interrupting
>
> Insisting on being right
>
> Blaming
>
> Teasing
>
> Overstepping boundaries

There are many games and lessons teachers can use to help children avoid these problems and connect with other children and adults.

Exclusion

In every part of life, the theme of exclusion raises its ugly head. This is because of the following fact: Human beings have a fundamental need to be accepted by others.

Once basic survival needs are met, the next most important thing in life to a human being is the need to belong, and to be accepted. Not being accepted or feeling one is not accepted can lead to terrible consequences – deep feelings of anger and abandonment can lead a person into depression or crime.

Bullying can wreak havoc on a school and destroy lives. We have all read what can happen to an individual child's self esteem when he or she is subjected to bullying in school, and not protected by adults or the system. It is vital to begin early work in a classroom setting in order to avoid the all too human tendency of people to exclude others. Here is a class I teach:

Exclusion

First I draw this picture on a chalkboard or paper on an easel:

When I draw this picture, children get very quiet. I work with children as young as 2 and as old as 5, and at all ages there is instant recognition of what is implied in this picture, though of course older children can verbalize more. This is an example of what happens in a class of 3-year-olds.

Q: What do you see?

A: She's over on this side, and they are over there.

Q: How do these two feel?

A: They're happy. They are beside each other. Their heads are together.

Q: How does she feel?

A: She's sad.

Q: Why?

A: Because there's no room for her in the middle. Because she can't fit in.

Q: Why is she sad?

A: Because she has to be all by herself.

Q: Why is that sad?

A: Because they don't see her. Because she wants to play. Because they are not talking to her.

Q: Why do you think they are not talking to her?

(This question often makes children stop and puzzle. They can't quite figure out how to think about what other people may be thinking – this is a skill that develops around the age of 4. However, or goal is to encourage even young children to speculate about the fact that people have motives behind what they do.)

A: Because they don't want to play with her.

Q: Why don't they want to play with her?

A: Maybe her head is too big. (I may have drawn one head bigger than the others!) Maybe she doesn't know what game to play. Maybe she is sad and that's why they don't want her to play. Maybe she is not their friend.

Q: What could she do?

A: She could squeeze in the middle of them. She could ask them if she could play. She could share her toy with them. She could say 'That's not fair'. She could say 'You hurt my feelings'. She could tell the teacher.

Here are some further questions I tend to ask an older group of children of say 4 or 5.

Q: Do you know what it's called when people do this? (pointing at the two girls together).

A: They are leaving her out.

Q: Yes that's right, it's also called EXCLUDING. They are excluding her. She feels excluded.

I write the word EXCLUDE on the board. This gives children the time to process the fact that there is a name for this feeling and this action, and that it is a universal experience, they are not alone when they feel this feeling. I use a new word so they can remember that they have a name for what they feel and they are learning new things about themselves.

Q: Do you know why some people want to stick together and exclude someone else?

A: They are afraid of her in their game.

Q: What do you mean?

A: If she comes over they won't be able to play together any more.

Q: I see, so they are playing together and she will take one friend away from the other?

A: Yes.

Q: So they are afraid they will lose each other or their fun will be over if they let this other girl in?

A: Yes.

Q: So people exclude other people because they are afraid?

A: Yes.

Now I take two other teachers and I act out a scene. In this scene, we play out the situation that was discussed. One of us is excluded and the other two huddle together and decide they will not let the third person in. The children often become quite distraught and call out things like:

Don't do that! That's not fair! You should be nice to her!

We replay the scene and this time we give the child who is excluded a voice, saying things like:

> *- I want to play with you.*
> *- Can we all be friends?*
> *- I would like to play in your game.*

In the end, the two excluders realize that they can find a role for her in their game after all. This way the children see that if a person speaks up they can find a way to resolve their problems instead of giving up and leaving.

Why it worked

Drawing a picture and allowing children to make their own inferences is a way of having them think about a situation, rather than being didactic and telling them there is a problem, asking them what they perceive is a way to help them problem solve. Asking children why they think the other child is excluded makes them think about motivation. Thinking about other people's motivation is a skill children need to develop so that they do not feel victimized. Knowing that a person is excluding you because they are needy and lonely themselves is empowering.

Giving a child words to use or techniques to respond to children when they are feeling left out, will prepare them for this situation when it happens again. Acting out the scene in which children have a solution to the problem gives them a script and a vision of how they can respond if they are excluded.

$$\ast \ast \ast \ast \ast \ast$$

Identifying feelings

A child is a boat bobbing on a sea of emotion. In order to learn navigational skills, a child must understand the currents, and watch for storms. Teachers need to help children to know what they are feeling.

During the day-to-day moments that occur in a classroom, a teacher can step in and interpret for a child. This is a situation that happens a lot so let's look at how it would work in a classroom where the teacher is committed to Emotional Education:

Your lunch is yucky!

It is lunch time. The children are seated at table and starting to eat the lunches they have brought from home. Some have sandwiches, some have pasta, rice, chicken, seaweed, and so on. Jeremy has a bowl of pasta with pesto and it has a strong smell of basil and garlic. He is getting ready to dig in, it's his favorite lunch.

JENNY: Ooh what's that smell?

JEREMY: That's pasta, my mommy made it.

JENNY: Why is it green?

JEREMY: It's pesto.

JENNY: That's yucky!

Jeremy stops smiling. He hangs his head. Everyone keeps on eating. Jeremy just ignores the comment and starts to eat. The teacher sees this and feels bad. She can tell that Jeremy has some reaction to Jenny's comment. She wonders what is the right thing to do. Do children have the right to say what they think? Is it OK for

Jenny to express her dislike of pasta with pesto? Should the remark go unnoticed? Should she ignore the fact that Jeremy might feel bad? Should she cut into their lunchtime and say something?

THE SOLUTION

The teacher realizes that though this might seem like an innocuous phrase, a child just saying what she thinks, it is actually hurtful to the other child, and it is her job to be instructive and teach the children the right thing, even at lunchtime. She knows that having someone call your lunch yucky can make a child feel excluded from the group, because he will assume that everyone thinks his lunch is yucky. And she knows that the child who doesn't like pesto doesn't have to like pesto, but needs to learn an important lesson that her words can affect others. So she steps in.

TEACHER: Jenny do you not like pesto?

JENNY: Eww no!

TEACHER: Have you ever tasted it?

JENNY: No!

TEACHER: I see, you just think that you would not like it, right?

JENNY: I would not like it.

TEACHER: Jeremy, you like it, though?

JEREMY: I like it.

TEACHER: Your mommy made it for you, right?

JEREMY: Mmm.

TEACHER: Can I ask you a question?

JEREMY: Mmm.

TEACHER: Did you like it when Jenny said your lunch was yucky?

JEREMY: *No, I didn't like that. (Now he frowns. He seems to be realizing for the first time that he did have a feeling.)*

TEACHER: *Jenny, did you know that Jeremy didn't like when you said that?*

JENNY: *But I don't like it!*

TEACHER: *Yes, I know. Some people like pesto, and some people don't. Some people like peanut butter, some people don't. Everyone likes different things. But I think Jeremy likes what his mommy made for him, and he says that he didn't like when you called it yucky. Maybe you could just say that YOU don't like it. When you call something yucky it might hurt his feelings. Did that hurt your feelings when she said it was yucky?*

JEREMY: *Yes, I didn't like that!*

TEACHER: *I'm sure Jenny didn't know it would hurt your feelings, she didn't mean to hurt you, did you Jenny?*

JENNY: *No I didn't. I just don't like it. I don't want it.*

TEACHER: *That's ok, you don't have to like it, but we need to remember that our words might hurt other people. And Jeremy, I would like you to be able to say to someone: 'That hurt my feelings,' if you want to.*

JEREMY: *That hurt my feelings*

TEACHER: *I think Jenny knows that now, I am sure she did not mean it. I think Jeremy still likes you and you still like him, isn't that right? (They look at each other and laugh.)*

Why it worked

Children, and adults, often say things without realizing their impact on others. The teacher in this case was trying to teach children that people need to be observant about how our words impact others.
She was trying to do this by:

- Being reflective, stating the obvious, pointing out both sides of the issue and the fact that each child had certain emotional reactions.

- Giving words to a child who had covered up his feelings, and in this way speaking up for him and showing him that he has the right to say how he feels.

- Validating that the child who dislikes a certain food has the right also to express her dislike in a constructive way.

Giving children the words in which they can express negative feelings: 'I don't like pesto' and 'That hurt my feelings,' are both expressions of feeling while being neutral. Children feel very empowered when they learn that they can say "That hurt my feelings." It's not hurtful or reactive, it's just a statement of fact. Stating your feelings is always the most respectful way to say something, because it means you are accepting responsibility for the fact that you know it is your feeling, it's not accusing the other person.

Teachers need to prevent the development of bullying – whether it is intentional or not – by stepping into situations like this and rather than taking sides, giving instruction, feedback and guidance on how feelings can be fairly and responsibly expressed.

Expressing Feelings

Let's Call your Mom Right Now!

A group of 3-year-olds are gathered for their emotional lesson. They come into my room and sit around the edge of a square rug, while I sit at the front with an easel, paper and markers. In this setting, before we get to work on our emotions, I make sure everyone is sitting at the edge of the square rug, and I do not start until everyone is in place around the edge of the rug, which I tell them is called 'the perimeter'.

NOTE ABOUT BOUNDARIES: *The reason I take time making sure everyone is sitting in place, is not to be strict, or to make sure they are 'well behaved.' The reason I take these few minutes to organize the children and have them settle into a specific space, is to set boundaries. I do this for the following reasons: First of all, everyone is sitting on the perimeter, so each child can see clearly, no one is sitting in front of anyone else. There is no choice for them to make about where they should sit. When there is no choice, this relieves the child of any anxiety about making a decision as to where they will sit. It may seem counterintuitive, but having a boundary can make a child free to think and process feelings.*

Secondly, having boundaries provides a sense of emotional safety – we are going to discuss emotional issues and that can be very exciting, or anxiety-producing, so having limits and knowing someone is in charge helps children to feel safe.

Now the work begins. I look around the room, and notice that one girl has a serious expression. She looks somewhat sad and angry, and yet she is making eye contact with me which seems to indicate that she wants to be noticed. Her facial expression shows a real feeling, yet it is a dramatic expression which seems to say: 'I don't feel anyone notices me, I wish they would.' I say to the children:

"Hmmm, I am looking around the room and I see that one person looks a bit like this…" I begin to draw. I draw a simple circle shape to represent a face, taking my time, since the children are very engrossed now, they don't know who it is going to be. Drawing slowly and taking my time helps the children to become more thoughtful about what is happening. I draw two circles for eyes with two more circles inside turned down and to the left, a line for a mouth that is straight but with a slight downward curve, and the eyebrows curved down slightly.

I say: "How do you think she is feeling?" and they say: "Sad." "Mad." A very emotionally aware girl calls out: "It's Eleanor." I say: "Yes, actually, that is who I was drawing. Is it OK if I draw you, Eleanor, I did notice your face looking like this?" and she nods. If she had said no I would not have proceeded. I was correct. She did want her feelings to be acknowledged.

"Let's talk about the kinds of things that make a person sad or angry," I say, and the children are all ready to talk:

"If you miss your mommy that would make you sad."

"You maybe got hit by someone."

"Someone took your toy."

"You don't want to go to school."

"There is no one to play with."

"Last night I didn't want to eat my dinner and I got mad."

"I hit my mommy and she was really mad and then she said it was OK and then we hugged and I wasn't mad any more."

The stories start to flow so I stop them and I say:

"That's good. So I hear you saying that everyone gets sad sometimes, and everyone gets mad sometimes. Now let's see if we can find out what is bothering Eleanor. Eleanor, I am not sure if you are sad or angry. Do you know?"

"Sad," she says. "And angry."

"Good," I say. "People can have two feelings. "Do you know why you feel this way?"

"I miss my mommy," she says. "And she didn't say good-bye to me this morning, she left and I was at the window and she forgot to wave." She folds her arms and scowls.

"Oh no!" I say. "Did you tell the teacher?"

"No," she says.

"Why not?" I asked.

"Because I just wanted to be by myself."

"OK," I say. "But you are still sad, so your feeling did not go away. Do you want me to call mommy now and tell her how you feel?" She nods. I pick up a toy car that is sitting on the table and I talk into it as if it is a telephone.

"Hello. Can I talk to Sylvia?" I say. The children smile. Eleanor's eyes widen. She is smiling. "Sylvia, is that you?" I say. "I just want to say I'm a little mad at you. You know you forgot to say goodbye to Eleanor this morning. I don't like that!" There is a big roar of laughter from the children, including Eleanor. "Eleanor was waiting for you at the window, and you did not look back. I am going to send you to your room!" Another roar of laughter. "Yes, I know you were in a hurry but Eleanor wanted to say good-bye. That's it! Go to your room!" Laughter. "And don't come out until you are ready to say sorry." Laughter again.

I look around the room. Everyone is happy, laughing, excited.

"Is there anything else you want me to say to mommy?" I say to Eleanor.

"Yes. Tell her again that she didn't say good-bye." I repeat the game. Over and over, each time to a resounding cheer. Then I start to get requests from the audience.

"Call my mommy. Tell her I don't like going to bed." I pick up the 'phone' again and I protest on the child's behalf.

"Mommy, I don't want to go to bed. I'm never going ever ever again! You go to bed and I will stay up!" Laughter.

For the rest of the session the children have their grievances aired. Someone doesn't like peanut butter sandwiches. Someone else wants to eat candies for lunch. My phone calls to their parents open up a world of possibilities where they can say what they want and have what they want.

At the end of the lesson I return to Eleanor, whose sad and angry face started the whole discussion. "Eleanor," I say, "what do you want me to say to your mommy now. Do you want me to be mad with her again?"

"No," Eleanor says. "Tell her I miss her."

"Mommy I miss you," I say. "I can't wait to see you again when you pick me up. Please don't forget to wave next time." I look at Eleanor.

"Is that what you want to say?"

"Yes." She says.

"Do you feel a little better now?" I ask.

"Yes."

Eleanor does not want me or anyone else to stay angry at her mother. She loves her mother and just wants to express a temporary feeling, so it's important to acknowledge that. To let her have her feelings, and to work through them. At the end of the day I tell her mother that Eleanor missed her, and that we played a pretend game where she told her she was mad at her for not waving at the window.

Eleanor's mother feels guilty about it, but we talk about the fact that it's fine, Eleanor feels very loved and knows that she will always be there for her, we are all human, and the love between a parent and child is not so fragile that one little forgotten wave can change that.

I tell her that it is a sign of emotional strength for Eleanor to be able to express these feelings openly, and a tribute to her good parenting. It is important to disclose to parents what a child has been feeling, and to remember that a parent will have a reaction to their child's feelings also. This particular mother is wonderfully able to accept her child's expression of feelings and she knows they will grow close to each other because of it.

Why it worked

What is the point in this lesson? Is it teaching children to be disrespectful to their parents? Is it encouraging children to be grumpy or negative? Is it sowing the seeds for anarchy? NO. The point in this lesson is that young children often have these feelings:

- I am small and everyone else is big

- Someone big makes the rules and I always have to obey

- I don't always get what I want

- No one listens to me

- When I get mad I say angry things and I am told to not say them

- I wish I could be in charge

- I wish I could do everything my own way

So of course children can NOT do everything their own way. They can't eat candies instead of lunch. They have to deal with rules, they have to accept reality. They need to go to bed every night, whether they feel like it or not. But what they can do, and have a right to do, is to express their feelings about following the rules.

They need to be allowed to say I don't WANT to go to bed. They need to be able to say I WISH I could have candies. They need to be able to say I am ANGRY that I can't have my way. Many people do not realize that just being allowed to say what you feel makes the feeling tolerable and is the best way for you to accept what you don't like.

Being made to do something and not being allowed to voice your feelings about it may cause resentment. It's like when someone jumps into a pool of cold water, just yelling out a loud scream makes it more bearable.

So the point of the lesson is that I am – in a safe space and in a very playful way – giving a voice to the children's unspoken wishes. They wish they could stay up all night with their parents. They wish they could rule the world. They wish they could have whatever they want whenever they want. By airing out those grievances, the children feel a sense of relief.

They also see how ridiculous it is to wish to never go to bed. They laugh when they hear about the child sending the mother to her room, they know it's not appropriate because the parent is rightfully the one in charge. Their laughter means they see the absurdity of getting all your wishes. Deep down they know their parents are right, and that the rules are for their own good. They just want the chance to express their feelings.

Teaching a child good communication skills

Children are not born able to communicate – in fact all they have when they are born is a great pair of lungs and the instinct to cry when something is wrong.

Vocal Exercises

Children need to learn how to be in a group, how to get along, how to understand, and how to get their needs met. They need to know that they have tools and assets which help them to socialize. One of their most important tools is their voice. Children can learn not only to analyze social situations and figure out what they are feeling, as well as what others are feeling. They can learn how to communicate in an effective way.

Some of the vocal habits which can sabotage a child's healthy communication with their family and friends are:

Whining

Complaining

Speaking too quietly or not at all

Yelling and interrupting

One way to help is to teach children how to use their voices. Here are some exercises children love:

VOWELS:

Teacher writes A E I O U on a blackboard or chart. She draws the shapes for each vowel that a child will use to shape the mouth: Square, flat rectangle, long rectangle, circle, small circle. Children are encouraged to shape their mouths as they pronounce each vowel.

VOLUME:

First lesson can focus on one vowel, say A. Teacher will draw a curved line of vowels increasing in size. Children will work on volume, from soft rising to loud and back to soft again:

Children enjoy being allowed to be loud. But they also are learning to bring their volume back down, and gain control over their voices.

PROJECTION:

The teacher can draw a bouncing ball, and the children can learn to make a staccato or choppy sound – A A A A. They can place their hand on their diaphragm and learn how the diaphragm works to push out sounds.

TONE and PITCH:

The teacher will demonstrate that a vowel can be low and rumbling or high pitched, and she can draw a tiny bird or a big bear and make her voice go from deep toned to high pitched.

EXPRESSION:

OHH!   UH-OH!   OH NO!

The teacher will draw children's attention to the emotional impact that he or she can create with the voice, using facial and body expressions for emphasis. For instance the letter O can be used in surprise: OHH! (smile, raised eyebrows) Or in anger: OH NO! (with a frown or arms folded) Or in humorous reprimand to a naughty puppy: No! No! No! (wagging the finger). Or in shock: UH OH!

There are many variations a teacher can bring into this work. The teacher can draw the class's attention to the ways in which we communicate, and can talk openly about communication problems such as whining, complaining, low tone, fear of asking to join the group.

✳ ✳ ✳ ✳ ✳ ✳

Emotional Lesson: How to ask for what you need

A Child has a Voice

Children should be taught about the power of the voice to express feelings and to communicate feelings. Interpreting the tone of someone's voice is a natural ability children have, they understand the emotional nuances of music instinctively. You can see how even a small baby reacts to a sweet high tone of voice and will recoil from a harsh or loud sound. Teaching children about their voices has many benefits:

- It helps them to be assertive

- It helps them to make friendships

- It helps them to use their voice to present their feelings clearly

- It helps them to convey negative feelings in an acceptable way

- It helps them to obtain release for deep feelings

- It helps them to understand how others can be influenced with vocal tone

Teachers can conduct vocal exercises that help children understand the full range of the human voice and the potential they have for communicating in a clear and acceptable way. In addition they can address some of the vocal problems that children can encounter when they are trying to join a group or have their needs met by children or adults. Some of the vocal habits which can sabotage a child's healthy communication with their family and friends are: whining, complaining, low tone or shyness, or yelling/interrupting.

Teachers can help with these issues, here are some ideas of how vocal exercises can work.

Whining

Many parents complain about their child whining. It irritates them and makes them want to not give in to the child. They often say they are completely frustrated by whining and just don't know how to stop it. Their frustration makes them say things they don't mean things that don't really make sense, such as: "I can't hear you when you use that voice," which is untrue. They do that to try to manipulate the child and stop the whining. The thing is, a child whines when she does not feel able to ask for what she needs. Whining is a result of a feeling of helplessness. If children don't feel helpless, they won't whine. We must remember that children have the right to ask for things they need. They don't always get to have what they want, but they should be allowed to ask in any case. Here are some examples of how we work on whining and transform it into healthy assertiveness:

Let's all Whine Together!

Children are sitting at the snack table and are eating snack and drinking water. A child calls out in a whiny pathetic voice: "I have no water...I have no water.." This tone almost automatically creates a feeling of irritation in the listener. The teacher wants to say: "Stop whining!" But that would be to fall into a pattern of behavior which does not get to the root of the problem. So here is a game which is more helpful for children:

Assertiveness vs. Whining

The teacher uses two puppets and shows the children how to ask for what they want without whining. The first puppet says in a (heavily dramatized) whiny voice: "I didn't get any snack. Not fair...I didn't get any snack..." When the teacher does this, children laugh. They recognize the tone, and the laughter is recognition.

The second puppet says: "Teacher can I have a snack please?" When asking like this, the teacher models a strong, assertive voice. Children do not have to be sugary sweet when asking for what they want, they just need to use an assertive voice that is pleasant to hear, because they have the right to ask for what they feel they need.

We tell the children: You have permission to ask for what you need or want. The answer will either be yes or no, but we are here to help you, or to tell you how you can get what you want. We won't give you something that is dangerous, but we will always listen. You do not need to complain, you need to ask. And sometimes you can get it yourself.

Once again the scene is played over again, and this time the teacher asks the children to whine along: "I didn't get any snack...." The children enjoy practicing whining. This helps reinforce what whining is. Then we switch over: "I need some snack please. Can I have snack please?" In this way children learn not to whine, but to be assertive.

Complaining

Children often complain instead of identifying their own needs. This is symptomatic of passivity, which will not help the child in his or her life. Many people grow up to be complainers. They write letters to the newspaper, they gossip about other people, they feel the whole world is against them. But there are other people, who, when they recognize a problem, decide they are going to do something to help solve it. Those people become leaders, movers and shakers, high achievers. They are also creative people who, when they identify a problem, see it as an opportunity. We want children to be able to identify problems and not be overwhelmed by them. How can we do that? By teaching them healthy assertiveness.

The point of this exercise is to have children realize that they should communicate their needs directly, and that they will always be listened to if they ask for what they want. This is not an occasion to instill manners or enforce the use of the word please. Before we discuss the exercise I would like to make a point about the word 'please.'

The word 'please' and the social contract

First of all, don't get me wrong on this, I think the word 'please' is a lovely word. I use it a great deal, in fact I almost always say it when I ask for anything from anyone. And I say 'thank you,' a great deal. Because these words imply a social contract. The social contract I speak of is that no one owes anyone anything. We all live together with our various needs, emotions and problems. And our social contract implies that we agree to live together as peaceably as possible, and in order to do that, we agree to understand the difficulties other people have.

So when someone does something helpful we say 'thank you,' on the understanding that they do not have to do it. We say 'please' because we know that others do not have to help us, and we need to be respectful when we ask that they do. These social graces help to bond us to each other and create an atmosphere of what we call civility, or we can also call it kindness.

Parents and teachers – rightly – work hard to pass on those social graces to children. We teach children to say 'thank you' when a waiter brings us food, or when someone opens a door for us. We teach them to say 'please' when they are asking for something from others, such as when they are in a store, or at table, for instance: 'pass the milk, please.' It is a very nice thing, and it does serve the child well in the sense that it endears adults to children when they are asked respectfully for something.

However, I have to say that although the word 'please' is very important and should be taught to children, the following exercise is one in which I do not enforce children to use this word, for a good reason. The reason is that I believe children have the right to ask for what they need, simply because they are dependent on us. If someone is dependent on you, then forcing them to say 'please' every time you fulfill their basic needs is not necessary or desirable. You can teach them to use a pleasant tone, to respect your needs, but you should not force them to beg for their basic needs. Please see the exercise to follow my point.

✳ ✳ ✳ ✳ ✳ ✳

The difference between complaining and assertiveness

There's no milk in my cup!

We are sitting at snack table. A child calls out in a distressed way:

"There's no milk in my cup!" This kind of complaint can make an adult irritated or uncomfortable because it is passive/aggressive. There are two possible responses the adult can give to this, defense or attack:

1. I'm sorry I didn't go fast enough...here you go

2. Don't speak to me like that, it's rude, say please

Either of these two responses will move the problem out of the way and satisfy the child's need for milk. But this is school, after all, and we are all about Emotional Education. And this is a perfect opportunity to teach the child about complaining. What the child is doing is stating the problem, but in a needy way, and that can best be described as complaining.

In the first response when the teacher fills the child's cup, he is reinforcing the child in the habit of complaining – if you complain then you will get things done. In the second response, he is changing the child's habit from complaining to pleading – if you beg then I will help you. In both cases, the teacher is reinforcing the child's dependence on the adult. What is needed in the case of a child complaining, is for the teacher to help the child to be an active participant in the classroom, and in her own life. Here is the way we would help:

MARCY: *There's no milk in my cup! (whiny complaining tone)*

EILEEN: *I hear someone calling out loud. Is that you Marcy?*

MARCY: *Yes, there's no milk in my cup.*

EILEEN: *But who are you talking to? You are calling out into the air like this (I imitate Marcy and yell out without focus.) There are three teachers here, and no one knows who you are talking to, so you might not get what you are looking for. You need to pick one of us, which one do you want to help you?*

MARCY: *You.*

EILEEN: *Then this is what I would like you to say:
'Eileen I need milk.'*

ANGELA: *She should say 'please.'*

EILEEN: *I don't mind if she says please or not, as long as she tells me what she needs. Please is nice to say, of course. Go ahead, Marcy, practice it.*

MARCY: *(shyly) Eileen.*

EILEEN: *Yes?*

MARCY: *I need milk.*

EILEEN: *(rushing over) Yes, of course! Milk for you! Anything for you!*

MARCY: *(with a very pleased expression) Thank you.*

Why this works

This solution teaches the child to identify an adult who can help them, rather than venting a problem aimlessly. When a person is asked for a favor by name, he or she is much more likely to respond than when someone complains to the general public. Try this yourself, if you ask a person by name for a favor, you will see that person will be much more likely to help you. Secondly, it teaches the child that she has the right to ask for what she needs and to be open about her neediness.

This is a very valuable lesson in life. How many adults would feel comfortable saying to their life partner "I need you to hold me?' or 'I feel needy right now?' How much better our lives would be, if we could do so. Why do we feel we can't call on one another in our times of need? Why do we feel we have to hide our neediness? It all begins in childhood, and that's why we should allow children to express their needs openly.

Another possible solution would be this:

MARCY: *There's no milk in my cup!*

EILEEN: *Marcy, there is no milk in your cup?*

MARCY: *No!*

EILEEN: *Where is the milk?*

MARCY: *It's at the other end of the table.*

EILEEN: *What do you think you could do?*

MARCY: *(puzzled expression) I don't know*

CHILD 1: *She could go over and get it.*

CHILD 2: *She could ask me to pass it to her.*

EILEEN: *There you go, Marcy, what would you like to do?*

MARCY: *Could you pass it over.*

CHILD 2: *Here it is.*

MARCY: *Thank you.*

Why this works

This solution shows Marcy that she can take action to help herself. She can get up and fetch the milk without waiting for permission. It also shows her that she has other help right around her, her friends who are ready and willing to assist. There is always help at hand, and teaching a child to reach out to others rather than sink into helplessness, is another way of building resilience and community.

The point about whining and complaining is that it's a passive reaction to a problem. In the above examples, an adult can point out to a child that he or she can speak in an assertive way and ask for what is needed. Or the adult can give the child the solution to the problem, point out where the resources are, and enable the child to find his or her own way to the resources. There's an old saying about giving someone a fish versus teaching them how to fish for themselves. That applies here, except when we hear someone whining about fish, we give them permission to go fish!

Building a child's emotional vocabulary

Discovering Transference

> *This is another story about Wallace, the same boy we started the book with. Wallace joined our program when he was 2 years old, and from day one he was a very emotionally open boy. He would smile so broadly when he was happy that his face truly cracked from one ear to the other, while his eyes widened and sparkled – he was full of life. He was very creative, and he would be so excited by a game, something that he imagined or invented, that he would play for long periods of time either alone or with others, and often he would have to almost be dragged away from it.*

> *Wallace would fly easily into tantrums, his face turned red, he would quite easily throw something against the wall, or stamp away, when things didn't go his way. He was not mean to others, but his anger could flare up like a wildfire. His feelings showed in all he said and did. But he was not fragile. He learned to give and take*

and though he was embarrassed, he would go back and say he was wrong, and he really grew through the three years he was with us.

Wallace and I were very close. We engaged in verbal sparring during the time of his schooling. We were able to say I HATE YOU to each other, and we both knew we didn't mean it. We were able to say I LOVE YOU and both of us knew we did mean it. Each of us knew – he instinctively, me after years of study and therapy – that being angry is a normal part of caring about someone. Towards the end of his time with us, Wallace was four years old and I observed the following incident, which was gratifying. It proved to me that our program of Emotional Education can have a huge and lasting effect on children, and their families.

It is almost lunchtime. Wallace is coming up the stairs with his class on their way back from recess. I know that he is having a rough day, because I saw him at drop-off having a little meltdown. And I heard from the teachers that he had a few more difficult moments after that during the course of the morning. At recess I watched the class in the backyard, and I saw him sit by himself a few times. The teacher told me that he sat out of the group because things weren't going his way. I cared about how he felt so I walked over to him and asked what was going on and he said:

"I just want to be by myself right now." So I said:

"That's a good idea," and I left him alone. Now I am watching him as he is coming in for lunch.

As he goes up the stairs a little girl steps ahead of him unintentionally and he yells:

"Marcy!! You're so annoying!" Marcy turns around and looks puzzled and upset. Her eyes seem to be filling with tears, which she is fighting back. They reach the top of the stairs and are sitting on the bench, taking their shoes off before going into class. I see Wallace pouting and frowning, and Marcy is looking upset too, she's grimacing, looking around for help. Since I am right there, Marcy looks at me and says:

"It's not fair!"

"What's not fair?" I say

"Wallace just yelled at me for no reason!" Wallace turns around.

"You pushed ahead of me!" he says.

"I didn't know you were in front," Marcy says. "You shouldn't yell at me!" I look at Wallace. He is sitting on the bench looking very serious. His hands have forgotten to take his outside shoes off.

"You look upset, Wallace," I say. "You yelled at Marcy. I don't know what you are feeling, I can't tell if you are angry, I think the best word to describe your face is upset. I wonder what is happening with you?"

"He's mad at me!" Marcy says. "But I didn't know he was in front. I didn't." Wallace is very quiet for a minute. And then he looks at Marcy and says:

"I'm not mad at you." His face seems to lose its angry expression. "But I was mad at you when I was on the stairs."

"You were mad at her on the stairs?" I say. "When did you start getting mad at her?" He pauses, he's thinking deeply now. And then he surprises me by saying:

"Well, actually, I think I am not mad at Marcy at all. I think I was mad before I went on the stairs."

"Oh, really?" I say.

"I think I was mad at my mom this morning on the way to school. Maybe that's why I yelled at Marcy."

I was amazed. I have just watched a process of self-awareness that I never expected from a child this age. If someone told me it could happen I would not have believed them. But there it was, unfolding before my eyes. I am so excited I say to Wallace:

"Wallace, good job! I am so glad you figured this out! I am proud of you. Do you know what this is called?" (Wallace comes from a family where parents value literacy, they use big words and do not 'talk down' to him, so I know he will love this new word, and every child loves to hear new words, especially when it relates to their own processes.)

"No," he says, eager to hear.

"It's called transference," I say. "Can you say that?"

"Transference," he repeats, relishing the new word. I explain:

"Transference means when someone gets angry at a person, but they are actually angry at someone else. The anger comes out at the wrong person." Wallace looks wide-eyed and he seems very happy I am praising him. I am also very happy because I know that many adults go through their whole lives not realizing they are transferring feelings of abandonment, anger or fear, on to others, but this child has made a giant step forward by realizing what is going on with his feelings. I tell his teacher what has happened, and she is also very surprised and proud, and she decides to incorporate this into the morning meeting.

When the children are gathered in a circle, she asks Wallace to tell his story. He tells all about his incident with Marcy, and he is delighted to say that he was not mad at his friend, but that in fact, he was mad about the fight he had with his mom that morning. And he proudly remembers that this is called 'transference.'

Expanding the lesson:

The teacher takes the incident and expands on it. She tells a story about when she was a little girl and her brother took her bike. She was very angry at him, but did not say anything. Later that afternoon, when her best friend came over to play and asked her if she wanted to go for a bike ride, she was still angry at her brother, and she snapped at her friend: "Go away I don't want to play with you!" When she was sitting all alone without a bicycle or a friend, she realized that she should not have yelled at her friend. It took a while to realize it, but the anger was all about her brother taking her bike.

The next day Wallace's mother tells me that he has brought his new word 'transference' home to share with his parents, and that he is very proud that he was praised for his insight into his own emotions. I discuss the term with his mother and she is very impressed also that her son – who of course will still continue to have tantrums and emotional highs and lows since he is still only four years old – has gained a valuable insight into how his emotions work.

This is an important story for all of the teachers. We realize that it is possible for a child who is only four to process the lessons we have given him and to have a light bulb moment that many adults never have. We know that this insight will help Wallace to manage his many powerful emotions without stifling or censoring them.

Chapter 9

TEN THINGS NOT TO SAY
TO CHILDREN

1. I know you're upset BUT...

The word 'but' or any other similar way of cheering up
your child and moving off the uncomfortable topic to something
else is a disqualifier. It means you are not really feeling your
child's feelings, or you are afraid to tolerate the idea that your
child is upset. You need to allow your child to have her sad or
angry feelings. That is called acceptance. Your child does not
need you to tell her that everything is going to be OK.
She needs you to help her to develop her own strategies of
coping when things are not OK. Which will happen.
It's called life.

2. We don't do that in our family/class.

Any kind of statement that implies a child is different or outside
an important group because of his behavior will create shame, a
feeling of exclusion, and anger at the group from which he is
excluded. A child needs to be accepted with all his faults.
A parent or teacher can say: 'I know you did not mean to do
that/I know you feel bad/I've done bad things myself/You can
help us to fix things," or some other way of showing the

147

child that he always belongs in the group and can find forgiveness there.

3. Don't say that word ever again.

Remember that you should always keep the doors of communication open. A word is just that to a child. Even adults say things they don't mean, and children often say outrageous things just to get your attention. Be ready to listen when a child says: I hate you. You can say: "What's the matter?" Or if a child is beyond reasoning you can say: "You seem very angry. I will wait until you calm down and we can talk." Censoring the actual words a child uses is not a good way to keep her telling you what's wrong. Later on you can explain how harsh certain words feel to hear, and suggest other more suitable ones.

4. Say you're sorry!

Forced apologies are not good. It's better to ask a child to reflect on WHY they did something rather than having her say something she may not feel just to make the problem go away. Take the time to go over the situation and help the child figure out how her feelings made her to do something she shouldn't.

5. I can't hear you when you whine.

Some parents and teachers are irritated by whining, complaining, or demanding, etc. They try to control the child's behavior by forbidding a certain tone of voice, and they act as if they can't hear it. That's just a way of trying to make problems go away by ignoring them, and that does not work! There are many ways to work with a child's continued patterns of whining or demanding. It involves training the child to assert him or herself in a healthy way. Pretending you don't hear is frustrating and unhelpful.

6. Don't make such a big deal out of it.

To a child some small failure or roadblock may be incredibly frustrating, simply because they do not have the life experience to know that there will be another time. They may literally think that a pancake cut the wrong way is the worst thing that ever happened to them, because it did not turn out the way they envisioned it. They don't know that you can try again and do things over. Telling a child not to make a big deal of it is like saying: "Your feelings are not valid. I can't relate to you."

7. If he bullies you again, just fight right back.

When children complain about bullying, it's natural to feel protective. But the best protection for children is to guide them towards understanding that when people bully others, the problem is with the bully. Teaching children to retaliate does not help anyone. Children who bully, are suffering from poor self-esteem, and it's never too early to teach your child to understand the motivation behind other people's actions. You can teach children to stand up for themselves using words that are not aggressive or provocative, phrases that diffuse the tension such as: "I am sorry you feel that way," or "Well, that is your opinion," and so on, or teach them to seek peer support, but encouraging aggression puts your child in danger.

8. I expect you to get 100% next time.

Putting your expectations on your child can be very damaging. Failure is an important thing to process, we can often learn more from 'mistakes' than from successes. It is also important for children to set their own goals. Many successful people hit a low point in mid-life, when they have everything they thought they wanted. They realize that their success is not really theirs, they were following their parents' dreams. They may have to start over with the support of a therapist, to discover their own dreams and re-inhabit their own lives.

9. Stop playing and focus on work!

To a child, play is the most important thing in the world. Studies show that children who play creatively and cooperatively develop strong cognitive skills. In addition, they develop mental flexibility and 'divergent thinking' which helps them find solutions outside the obvious. Work is a very important aspect of life, and that is why a child needs to develop a playful attitude to his work. Parents and teachers can make a game out of cleaning up toys, or play math games by sorting colorful buttons, or teach chemistry through cooking. People who love their work maintain a playful attitude all through their lives, and this playful attitude begins in childhood.

10. You made me so angry!

Children and adults alike need to accept responsibility for their own feelings. The proper way to convey anger is not to say 'you MADE me angry,' but to say: "I felt angry when you said that...I felt hurt/embarrassed/small/helpless etc...." Blaming other people for your feelings or your reactions is not the same as accepting responsibility for your reaction to something which happened. Blaming also shuts other people out. Real communication is when a person can show his vulnerability. A parent or teacher can show a child how to communicate his anger and understand the reason for it. We all face problems in life, and we all have feelings that we can't predict or change, but we can choose how we react to those feelings.

Chapter 10

CASE HISTORIES

The following are some case histories. They track the progress of some children who have attended our school, and who have benefited from our program. In other schools, some of these children might have been labeled as difficult, or dismissed from the program. Their spirit might have been crushed, or they might have internalized the idea that they were different, or bad. Labels such as these (which a child readily accepts) at an early age are very hard to unstick. In all of these case studies we worked actively with parents, and this school/home partnership has benefited the child and the family.

We understand that a child's first years are a difficult time for parents. Children can't communicate in words for the first and most formative period of their lives, and often have to resort to screams and tantrums to show their frustration and their deep feelings. Parents realize that it is their job is to control and guide children, and they often struggle with knowing whether they are too strict, or too lenient. A supportive school can help parents in this work. Many children spend almost as much time in school as with their parents, so this is a wonderful opportunity for us to work with parents as partners to help shape their children into happy individuals and group members.

We pride ourselves on the fact that we get very positive feedback from the schools to which our children graduate – they say they can tell how well our children are prepared for a classroom setting. Children cannot develop academically if they are struggling to get along with others, emotions can be distracting. The skills we teach in our school help children to manage their feelings and communicate them in a healthy way, and focus on their work. Here are some examples of the work we have done.

Colin and His Mother

Colin was a small 3-year-old boy, very quiet when he visited for an initial play date. He had not been to school before this, and his mother noted on the application that he was shy. At his first visit, he was accompanied by his mother and his older sister. His mother was a lovely, sweet and gentle woman who appeared nervous, and that nervous appearance was reinforced by her statements. Her first words were:

"He's very intelligent, but he's shy. I'm not sure how easy all this will be for him...I think he will be alright but he's very attached to me." As Colin stood at a close distance from his mother, watching children play with Legos at a table, his older sister spoke to the teacher:

"He's a bit shy," she said. Then she walked over to him and handed him some Legos.

"Here you go," she said. Colin took the Legos then started playing with them. The teacher came over to Colin and said:

"Would you like to come here and sit at the table? There are more Legos here." Colin reluctantly walked closer to the table. The teacher motioned to the mother to come closer, and as she came closer so did Colin. The play date went well and in the end Colin was not eager to leave. His first day of school was to be two weeks later, and that's when the trouble started.

On his first day, Colin's mother looked nervous when she brought him up the stairs and into the room. Her eyes were wide and her face was drawn, and anyone – including Colin – could see her distress. But that distress was nothing compared to Colin. He walked into the room behind her, holding on to her skirt. When it came time for her to leave, he protested, which is a normal reaction when a child is starting school, and his mother held back her own tears, barely, and left him in the care of the teachers.

When she was gone, Colin cringed against the wall. He looked like an animal, crouching, defensive, angry, ready to lash out. The teachers approached him with various techniques – showing him cool toys, asking him how he was feeling, wondering if he wanted a drink of water, trying to engage him in conversation. But he hissed and screamed at them like a wild creature and if they came close he made threatening gestures with his arms. The teachers decided it was best to leave him alone since that seemed to be the message he was sending.

Over the course of the day he would calm down and sit on the floor by himself, quietly watching the other children. But he became very defensive, making a scary face and sounds at anyone who approached. The other children just looked at him, they knew better than to approach him, but they would stand and observe him. He was very uncomfortable, and the teacher was worried about whether this was a good idea for him.

The teacher emailed his mother to let her know that he did well on his first day but that they should talk about him since he needed some support. They had a lengthy email exchange. The teacher asked his mother how SHE was feeling. His mother expressed a lot of worry and fear as well as a huge dose of guilt for leaving him, and yet she felt that he would somehow be able to adapt to school. When the teacher asked why she was so fearful, she could only answer that her father had died during the summer, that she was going through a lot of health issues, and that she was alone since her husband was on assignment in Europe.

The teacher listened patiently and responded to her concerns. She expressed understanding of how difficult this separation might be for the mother, since she had just lost her own father. Colin's mother seemed grateful for the acknowledgement of her feelings. She asked the teacher for suggestions on how she could help her son. The teacher suggested reading: "Everyday Goodbyes" – a book that

talks about separation, she had a copy and she would lend it to her.
The teacher also gently and tactfully suggested that Colin's mother
not show her distress on her face, but rather she should try to
present a calm and confident demeanor, no matter what she felt.

Next day, Colin was a little less stressed. His mother did not show
her worries so openly and she made a bright and breezy exit after
hugging Colin. But the same pattern repeated itself. Colin cringed in
the corner like a frightened animal. The teachers noticed that he
liked to hold on to a soft stuffed bear and they put it in the corner,
and made sure to tell him that was only for him, no one else could
use it. They noticed that he liked to sit on a little couch, and they
made sure to put that couch over in the spot where he had
crouched on his first day. They told him it was his cozy spot, and he
could use it any time he wanted. When it came to story time, he
didn't want to join the group, so the teachers told him that he could
choose between the group and the couch, and let him sit where
he wanted.

Things continued like that for a week or so. Some of the children
had been watching Colin, and one or two them asked why he was in
the corner, why he did not want to join the group, and so on.
At circle time the teacher asked if anyone noticed that Colin was
sitting off by himself, and she asked if they knew why. Some children
said that he missed his mother. Others said he was shy. And others
said that he didn't know anybody, and didn't have any friends.
All this time, Colin was sitting on his couch, listening to the
children, wide-eyed.

Then the teacher asked the children what they thought would help
him. They suggested that he might like to sit on the couch the whole
day, or that he might like some more stuffed toys, or that he might
like a hug, or he might like to be left alone, and some suggested
that he might like a book to read. As they made comments about
what they thought would help him, Colin listened to them with great
interest. He seemed happy to realize that he was the subject of
care and concern.

That evening, the teacher emailed his mother again, and asked what
Colin had said about school. His mother reported that he talked
about Legos. He told her that other children were playing with
Legos but he didn't. He told his mother that he liked the couch, but

he didn't like school. His mother was wise enough to know that he meant he didn't want to separate from her. She read him the book the teacher had recommended and he wanted to hear it being read over again.

After a couple of weeks, there was a noticeable change. Colin's mother smiled a lot, gave him a few big hugs and a wave as she left promptly, and this time when she left he did not cry. He still retreated to the couch with his pet bear but the teachers had placed the Lego table close to his couch, so he could see everyone playing and he could almost reach it from where he was sitting. The teachers did not come near him, deciding to let him find his own way gradually.

Sure enough, after a while he began to approach the Lego table. He stood beside it, watching everyone, and then he sat down and started to play. Soon, he began talking to one of the other children. The teachers just watched from the distance, delighted to see he was breaking through his resistance and beginning to make friends. At recess time, he became very engaged at the sand table, and he and another boy stood silently together pouring sand from one bucket into another.

The teacher shared the story of Colin's social successes with his mother, and she could tell that Colin's mother was feeling much more comfortable now, and not worried or guilty about leaving Colin. One morning, to everyone's surprise, he ran into the classroom and asked: 'where's the Legos?' The teacher said: "We didn't put them out, why don't you go get the box yourself and bring it over to the table." He knew where everything was, since he had been watching so intently, so he ran over and brought the box to the table.

He was becoming more a part of the class now, and taking ownership. Within a month, he was eager to participate in the class. The teacher suggested to his mother that he bring in something to share for snack. So he and his mother made muffins to share. The next morning, Colin was delighted to stand up in front of the group and talk about the muffins the children were about to eat. He explained how he and his mother had made them, and he had a list of the ingredients. The teacher asked the other children if they had questions, and he answered them. The children eagerly clapped at the end, and he smiled and blushed with excitement.

As time went by, Colin was clearly happy to come to school – by December he actually ran down the street and up the steps into school, leaving his mother behind him. She beamed with happiness, knowing he didn't feel afraid any more, and did not need to cling to her. But he still tended to 'clam up' when asked a question at meeting time, or at dance class when everyone else participated, he tended to hang back and stay close to the teacher. So the teacher decided to try to find something that he could bring to the group. She was searching for a way to help him feel he was part of it, and had something to contribute. She gave him the job of bell ringer. When it was time to clean up, he was to take the bell and remind everyone to clean up. He liked his job, because he could make a noise and be heard, and everyone did what he asked them to do.

The teacher discovered that Colin was an expert on the human body, he loved books about the skeleton, the heart, the blood, and so on. So she asked him if he would be willing to bring in some books on that subject, which he did. When she started reading them to the class, he quickly jumped in as she read: "It's called the HUMERUS!" he would yell out. "Your heart is the same size as your fist!" The teacher invited him to sit on the teacher seat beside her so children could ask him questions.

He loved talking about the interesting facts he knew about the human body. Pretty soon the other children looked at him as an expert.

At this point Colin had found a role in the group. He was the expert on certain things and he was looked up to by the others for that expertise. He still didn't know how to join in at play time, though, so the teachers had to coach him and give him skills. When a group of children were building with blocks together he would stand at the edge not sure what to say or do. The teacher intervened in a way that would not make him feel embarrassed. "Is that block going to fall over? Colin do you think we could add something on there? Try this one.." and handed him a block. In this way she helped him ease his way into the group, and say things like: "Maybe Colin has an idea…" to get him involved with the other children.

It took him a while to do this by himself. At times the teachers had to resist helping, to leave him in a state of unease where he was clearly trying to find a strategy to make friends and watch him find a way. But he did. He made friends with another boy who was very talkative, and soon Colin was talking to him. The teacher encouraged his mother to schedule a play date with this boy outside school. The play date helped him to grow his friendship. In school he liked to sit beside that boy, and they would make plans to play together at recess time. Though that boy did not come to school every day, Colin's play skills had developed, so he was able to find other friends and make plans with them too.

By the time June came around, Colin's friendships were strong, and he was excited to participate in group discussions. Colin left us and moved on to elementary school. His mother was very nervous that he might have a hard time readjusting to a new environment. However, he left with a lot of new skills. He had gained confidence in himself. He could be an expert on something and gain the other children's respect. He could also bond with another child and make a strong one-on-one friendship, which would serve him well in any school setting. He left us, transformed from a scared and defensive boy into a happy and sociable child.

Over the years, Colin has come back to visit us. In fact he often comes to read books to the children. His mother stayed in touch with us and tells us how he has taken the skills he developed at our school, the tools he gained with Emotional Education, and became confident of his own abilities. He plans to be a doctor when he grows up, and I am pretty sure he will do it!

Analysis of what worked for Colin

At the end of the year it was clear that a number of factors had helped Colin to enjoy school and make friends. Communication between parent and teacher helped to create a team that would work on the problem. Focusing on the parent's feelings was important in helping her develop coping techniques. The teacher made an effort to understand family issues, and that gave insight into the nature of the problem – Colin's mother was undergoing serious grief in her life and that affected her separation from her son. It was important for us not to force him, but rather to allow him to move at his own pace so the solution could unfold in an organic way. Once we did that, we could take time to understand what he needed – a cozy space, privacy, a soft toy.

This was almost like making a cocoon for him to rest in while he watched and waited until he was ready to join.

Another strategy that helped in this situation was to involve the other children so that he felt seen by the group, and that eased his fears. Being aware of details, and picking up cues from his sister and his mother about his love for Legos was helpful, so we could find a technique of getting him to be attracted into the class. We strategized by placing the toys within easy reach so he didn't have to go out of his comfort zone too far. But by far the most effective tool was the kind of acceptance that we practice - allowing him to be angry and defensive and not trying to reason with him or snap him out of it demonstrated to him that we liked him just the way he was.

Ben and his Father

When Ben came to visit our school initially, we could see that he had a problem keeping still. He was a 2-year-old boy, who ran from one toy to another, picking them up, dropping them, running to the next one, sometimes tripping and stumbling, then getting up again and moving on to the next thing. While this is a normal sign of excitement in a young child, we could see that he did not have good control of his body. His mother was a lovely, very alive and emotional woman, who expressed interest in having him at our school. As we observed him, we felt that he might have a hard time adjusting to school, where there are rules and boundaries. But then his mother said something that endeared us to her and Ben greatly. She said:

"I hate the school he is in! They told me that there is no place for a child like him in their school. He's a problem child, that's what they said. He is my son, I hate that they call him a problem." Her eyes filled up with tears and she said: "He's a good boy! He's very bright! I know he's not perfect. I just want him to be happy, and your school seems like such a happy place, not like that other one. I would love him to be in a place like this."

We happen to be familiar with that school. There is a lot of regulation, a lot of order, and children are expected to be compliant – to sit still, to walk in a straight line, to be quiet when they are asked to be quiet. We knew from experience that no, Ben's behavior was certainly not the other school's fault, it's just that they were not able to help Ben, that's all. They are not interested in emotional work. They just want to take care of children, keep them busy and return them safe to their parents at the end of the day, all good goals, but they are not capable of doing the work we do.

We took a look at Ben's lovely huge eyes that sparkled with life and excitement. Based on his behavior, and the story his mother told us about the other school, it was obvious to us that he was not going to be an easy child to deal with. We realized that yes, there were some issues that would take work, maybe a lot of work. But the idea that Ben was being called 'a problem child', that he was being rejected out of hand by this other school, was a challenge for us, and we like challenges! We asked ourselves: if we didn't help Ben, then who will? We accepted him in our program.

Sure enough, Ben was difficult. He had two sides. He would come into the room full of excitement, and his presence did light up the room. He was very interested in everything, and he knew a lot of things, about science, about nature, about buildings, about cars and engines. He was eager to talk about his interests, and his enthusiasm was so great that he could hardly contain himself at times, babbling away, talking loudly, his face red, his eyes sparkling. He was quite adorable, everyone noticed Ben and his larger than life personality.

But his problems soon manifested themselves. Ben had great difficulty with boundaries. He would march across the room to whatever he wanted to see, and seemed not even to notice anything in his way, inanimate objects or other children. He would barge by whole groups of children, brusquely knocking past, and would even knock toys over without stopping to see what happened in his wake.

At lunchtime he helped himself to other people's food. Though we tried to have him realize that he couldn't do that, as soon as we looked away, he would take something else. He didn't just take from the person next to him, he would even get up and go down to the end of the table, snatch something off another child's plate and run back to his place, stuffing the food quickly into his mouth before it got taken away.

We had to keep watching him because as soon as he felt like taking something, his hand would just reach out quick as a frog's tongue, and he would snap it up and put it in his mouth. It was strange to us, because he himself had the most delicious lunches lovingly prepared by his mother, which he also ate, along with his foraged samplings. He wasn't hungry or deprived. But he seemed to have no sense of awareness that he was stepping over someone else's boundaries by taking food off their plate.

At rest time Ben presented more challenges. We understand that at age 2 or 3 some children don't nap. About 80% of children do like to nap, but those who don't just lie quietly, talk to themselves, play with a soft toy, or read a book. Since most of the children do nap, those who don't are encouraged to relax, to be quiet. Ben was not just unable to relax, when other children napped he became agitated and did everything he could to disrupt things. The teacher would sit beside him, but he would sing loudly. When asked to be quiet he would do so, but then he would start kicking his feet against the floor, or make noise in some other way. When the teacher got up to attend to another child, Ben would jump up and start running around. It took all the teachers' energies to find ways of keeping him occupied so as not to disturb anyone else.

The interesting thing is that Ben was also very loving and very affectionate. He would run to greet the teacher in the morning, giving her a huge hug. He would participate at story time, contributing all kinds of wonderful comments that showed he was thoughtful and intelligent. He would try to be friends with the other children, but they were already distancing themselves from him because of his behavior. This created a vicious cycle, leaving Ben angry and frustrated. He would ask us why he had no friends. Ben was very lovable and very maddening! So we knew we had some work to do to transform this wonderful boy into a happier and more socially adept child.

The first thing we did was to connect with his mother. His father seemed to be in and out of the picture. We weren't sure if he was travelling his mother was the one who was most involved. We invited her in to talk. When she came in, her eyes were wide with anticipation. We could tell that she was just about ready to cry. And cry she did. She was hesitant at first, but when we told her we were worried about Ben's socialization, she broke down and told us the whole story of what was going on, in between bouts of tears.

Ben's father was suffering from severe PTSD. He had been conscripted into the army in a foreign country when he was younger, and he had experienced some traumatizing incidents. He had not processed these incidents, and at first, everything was great between the couple, in fact he never spoke about the past, about his time in the army. But unfortunately, as soon as he had a child, he began to relive his traumas. Because of that, his behavior had been very unpredictable lately, as his trauma seemed to be coming to the surface. He had been medicated at times, but at other times he had gone off the medication and his moods would swing back and forth. When he was depressed, he would want Ben to hug him and he would just hold the boy and cry. He would even wake Ben up at night and ask him for a hug. He was so emotional himself that he did not notice that Ben was scared, or worried.

Because of his father's fragile state, Ben's mother was stressed. As a result of the family dynamics, she felt she was the one trying to keep things together, and at times she would cry in front of her child. She was carrying the responsibility of caring for the father's emotions, managing her own anxiety, and supervising Ben, so the stress was enormous. And when Ben was running wildly, trying to forget his anxieties in crazy activity, she could not be calm enough to handle his behavior in a parental way. When he ran down the sidewalk she would yell at him or grab him by the arm or call him a bad boy out of sheer frustration.

She didn't feel good about herself – she cried with guilt when she told us how she yelled at her son. She knew it was not right, but she felt so burdened at times that yelling and grabbing was her only reaction. We helped her to feel good that she had shared this information and we said we would do all we could to support her and the family. Luckily, she was really open to help, and she and her husband were currently getting professional support for themselves to help them through the difficult times.

We realized that Ben had boundary issues because his father had overstepped his boundaries by being needy and unintentionally invasive. We knew that he was looking for attention in negative ways, and that he had poor self-esteem because his mother kept finding fault with him because of her own stress level. And we knew that he was having a hard time making friends because his own behavior was sabotaging him. We also felt that his behavior was not going to improve since he had already set up a bad dynamic with the other children, who avoided him at play time.

Our first step was to recommend that Ben talk to a play therapist. At times we know that this kind of intervention can be very helpful to a child. This one-on-one help, we felt, would support Ben while his parents were working on their own difficulties. The parents were grateful for the suggestion, and they did find a person to work with Ben. They also gave us permission to work with the therapist. She gave us feedback that Ben felt very lonely because the other children, he felt, did not like him, and he desperately wanted to belong. With that knowledge from the therapist, we began to work on finding ways for Ben to be accepted by other children. We knew that it was true, the other children had already begun to stay away from Ben because of his disorganized behavior.

One day I gathered a group of children together while Ben worked in another room helping the teacher prepare a snack. I told the group of children that I wanted to talk to them privately about Ben because I wanted to help him to be part of the group. I mentioned that I felt he had a hard time belonging in the group and that he needed us to support him. I asked them one by one to answer these two questions: "Do you like Ben?" and "Why?"

One by one they tried to answer honestly. Some said they liked him but they didn't want to play with him. Some said they did not like him because he hit. Some said they did not like him because he got into their space. Some of them said they did not like him because he would come by when they were playing with someone else and knock over their toys. Then I asked them: "Why do you think Ben does things like this?" There was a long silence. Children are not used to being asked to think why other people behave certain ways, so it is a skill they are only beginning to develop. Many adults don't even think of asking children to reflect on people's behavior.

Then Jennifer spoke up: "Maybe he has some feeling inside that makes him do that." I was very happy to hear this wonderful insight. I agreed that maybe she was right. Then a boy said: "Maybe he is hurting inside and it will never go away." I was so struck with this answer from a four year-old child. It made me proud of the work we were doing and awestruck at the ability of children to do this work with us. I agreed. "Yes, I think you are right," I said. "People do hurtful things when they are hurting inside."

"Why do you think he knocks over people's toys?" I asked. "Do you think maybe he wants to play with you and just can't find a way to ask, could it be that?" They agreed this was probably right. I prompted in this way because children may not be able to make this leap of thought at this age. "How can we help Ben?" I asked. They volunteered to be more friendly with him, to help him join in the group and not to leave him out. That conversation made a big difference, Ben began to be more accepted and his anti-social behavior diminished greatly.

When Ben was trying to join a group of children, we made sure to stand close to him and speak up for him. "Oh look, that's a nice building, maybe Ben has an idea that can help you," we might say. Little by little, Ben's behavior changed. He was getting the support of the therapist to whom he could confide his worries. His peers were beginning to let him into their play and he was able to play more constructively, he did not need to knock things over to get attention, he could get attention by showing his skills at play.

His confidence grew. Pretty soon he was bringing in books about topics he loved, superheroes, space, and so on. He was very happy to be accepted and listened to. The support he received from his therapist, from the teachers, and from his parents, worked together to help him overcome his anxieties and change his antisocial behavior. He finally started to take naps. It seemed like his defenses were down, he could trust people and feel able to relax into the space and into the group.

As time went by, Ben changed. In his next classroom, he still had difficulties, but the teachers stayed close to him, guiding him in his interactions. When he tried to enter into a group of children who were playing with blocks, they would tense up and try to corner him out. The teacher would speak for him: "It looks like Ben is here. I think he might want to play. Ben has good ideas. You'd like to play, right Ben?" Ben would nod, grateful for the help, and one child would say: "You can get a big block and put it here," and Ben would be delighted. If a problem arose, the teacher would say: "I see what's happening. Ben didn't ask anyone he just took that block away, is that why you're annoyed?" and Ben would be relieved to know it was just his actions they didn't like, not him.

Ben became less physical, his anxieties had diminished greatly so he didn't need to run around and distract himself from his feelings. He was now able to sit calmly and absorb what the teacher was saying, and the books she was reading. In fact, he became very attentive and his keen mind took in everything he was hearing. It was very gratifying to see him relax, to not be on guard and to be able to focus on work.

By the end of that year, Ben had a reputation among the children for building, designing, and generally having good ideas. His father, who was by now doing much better, came in to visit the class and showed them some architectural drawings, he was an architect and Ben was so proud of his father as the children all asked him questions about how buildings are made.

When Ben graduated from our school and went on to kindergarten, he was accepted in a private school, to which he would never have gained entrance a couple of years before. Those schools select individuals who are able to work well with others, and able to contribute positive energy to the group. By age 5, Ben was now able to sit still and listen when it was required, and his energy, instead of being destructive or self-sabotaging, was directed into projects. We heard back later from the exclusive school, that during his interview he talked at length about his ideas for building cars and rockets, and impressed the teachers there with his knowledge of how engines work, referencing some books we had read. We knew he had grown a great deal in the three years he was with us. Without the help and support he received from us and his therapist, he would have become the 'problem child' that he had been wrongly labeled at 2 years of age.

Analysis of what worked for Ben

Communication with parents was a vital part of this child's progress. Once we understood what the family was experiencing, it was possible to provide the support they needed. Secondly, knowing when professional help is needed is important – we need to know our own limits, and Ben had more problems than we could manage without intervention. The parents were open to having their child work with a therapist. Some parents worry that seeking professional help means there is something 'wrong' with their child. These parents were intelligent enough to know that it's ok to seek help, and they did not let their own egos or worries about what other people might think to get in the way. They were willing to show their needs to us, and to have their child receive the support he needed. Breaking the negative patterns Ben had set up with children involved a bit of intervention 'behind the scenes' so that the children could be part of the solution.

The school and the therapist worked closely together with the parents' permission, so we could interpret what Ben's behavior meant, and figure out what he needed most from us. We found that we needed to help the group interpret Ben, and Ben interpret the group. So every time he interacted, a teacher was there to coach him on how to integrate himself. Once he developed those skills, he felt more accepted. The more comfortable and accepted he felt, the more he could relax his body and sit and listen to stories, take naps, read books, and develop his interests. His mother was right, he was a very bright boy, but his emotional problems were getting in the way. Once he received help with his anxieties, fears, frustrations, and learned to set boundaries and respect boundaries, he could calm himself and be able to develop cognitively. It was hard work, but it was worth it to see a life transformed.

Francois and his Sister

Francois was a well-built, sturdy 2-year-old boy from France, who did not speak very much English. He had an older sister who was 6, and who did speak English, but Francois had spent most of his two years in France and was not at all fluent – he just blinked and stared at us when we asked him his name, and had to be prompted by his mother. But he did rush over and start to play with the trains and he spoke rapidly to his mother, clearly delighted to find all these fun things to play with, so we could see he was a happy, outgoing child.

He joined our school on the understanding that we would try to help him to communicate. We know that children learn new languages very quickly when they are very young. Our biggest worry in that regard is, that it's hard for a child to be part of a group where he does not understand what's going on, and he can't make himself understood. We know that can lead to a lot of loneliness and frustration. Still, he had a winning smile and a great spirit, and we felt sure that his positive nature would help him to thrive in a new situation.

But, things were more complicated than they seemed at first. Francois was a sweet lovely boy, he would sit with his eyes wide open, listening to stories, frowning a little, trying hard to follow along. When the class transitioned from one activity to another he picked up visual clues and knew it was time for snack, time to go outside, and so on. However, there was a serious problem. When he was playing on the floor with other children and he wanted a toy, he would just grab it out of their hand. If someone tried to take some thing he was playing with, he would scream loudly, and if the teacher didn't get there fast enough, he would swing his head around and open up his mouth, ready to bite the other child's arm, hand, whatever was closest.

That alarmed us. A bite can really hurt. It can break the skin. And it arouses a teacher's fears because it usually happens so fast that you don't see it coming. It is like a pure animal reaction. Our job is to protect everyone and when a child is prone to biting we have to be on the alert, especially if it 'comes out of nowhere,' which in fact it always does. The challenge here is not to overreact, but a teacher's first priority is safety, so we must stop a child from biting.

Very often you would hear a loud "FRANCOIS! STOP!" as the teacher ran to prevent him from hurting another child. When teachers did yell then Francois would recoil with a guilty look. He would cringe and look ashamed, like a dog that's been whipped. We realized that now, on top of his aggressive behavior he also had a self-image problem. We knew that he felt bad about what he did and that he also thought of himself as being bad, but there seemed to be nothing he could do to control himself. He clearly wasn't sadistic and wasn't out to hurt anyone, that's not who he was.

Within one month of watching and trying to manage this behavior, we realized that we would need to take action to help him otherwise he would soon be labeled as aggressive or unsociable, or he would hurt someone in a serious way. Besides, we could not continue to just yell STOP or assign one teacher to watch over him. So we began to work on untangling his problems. The first step was to give him the words in which to express himself so he did not need to bite, hit, or grab.

Normally we would speak to a child who bites and coach them on how to get what they want, how to speak to the other child. We would say things like:

"Tell him you want that toy"

"Say: I was playing with that"

"Ask him if you could have it when he is finished"

"Say STOP I don't like that!"

But in this case, Francois did not speak English. So the teachers were frustrated, AND they understood that Francois must be feeling very frustrated. It was time to connect with his parents.

The teacher brought his mother in for a meeting. She explained to Francois' mother that he got particularly upset if anyone sat too close to him, or took his toy away, or in any way made him feel put upon. And she mentioned that his English skills could use some reinforcement at home. His mother wondered aloud if his big sister was part of the problem. She often wrestled with him and one time he bit her, she told us. The teacher immediately realized that Francois might be feeling intimidated by her, and mentioned that to his mother. His mother agreed. She said that she sometimes put his sister in charge of him, and she wondered if that was the right thing to do, maybe she should not do it. The teacher agreed. Francois probably felt frustrated by having his sister 'push him around.'

They came up with a plan. The teacher would write a few phrases and words out for Francois' mother that she could practice with him at home. Her homework was teaching her son how to ask for what he wanted, and how to say STOP when he needed his sister to stop bothering him. She would also watch out for his needs for space and his right to be assertive.

For the next month, the plan was put into action. In school the teachers would speak out for Francois so he knew that he was not alone. This was done to show him that there was an authority figure he could rely on, and he did not need to defend himself or his toys by biting hitting or grabbing. For instance, the teachers might say:

"No, that's Francois' toy, he doesn't want to share it."

"Don't sit on top of Francois, give him some space."

"Don't shout at Francois, he doesn't like it."

"Please make room for Francois, he needs to sit down."

Secondly, the teachers would repeat useful expressions: 'give that back please,' 'I want to play with you,' 'you can have it when I'm finished,' when they saw a situation of conflict happening. They made him repeat these phrases so he could use them whenever he needed to.

In only a couple of weeks the biting stopped. Francois could be heard on his own trying out his phrases:

"Stop! I don't like that!"

"Can I play with that?"

"When you're finished can I have it?"

By December of that year, Francois looked more relaxed as he succeeded in having an effect on other children. He had discovered that when he said stop, they stopped. When he asked for a toy, they often shared it. When Francois did use phrases instead of being aggressive, the teachers praised him loudly, so he knew he was on the right track. He did not look so dour or so aggressive, he smiled a lot more, and the other children played with him more, and picked him out to be their partner, which made him happy.

In February, at the parent-teacher conference, his parents had a lot to report. They told the teachers that Francois talked a lot about school. He only spoke in English when he was talking about his teachers and his friends. And he was able to tell his sister "That's my toy," or "stop!" and they praised him for his assertiveness when he did.

By that point, the teacher reported to the parents, Francois' aggression had disappeared. They were happy to tell her that teachers did not need to watch him closely. They told his parents that he was very eager to listen to the books at reading time, and was excited to contribute his comments in halting sentences. The teachers repeated his comments, showing they understood him, and made him feel that he had something important to say.

By June, Francois was ready to move on to PreK, where he would be in a class of 20 other children and one teacher, instead of the small class of 12 and three teachers he was used to in our school. During his time at our school he had become prepared for this important transition. He had been helped to stop his aggressive behavior, which would not be accepted in a PreK class. He had been helped to communicate his needs and feel safe in a group. And he had been taught how to make friends with other children, to take turns, to wait, to ask for things, and to assert his boundaries.

On top of all this, his English language skills had grown very strong. This enabled him to progress to a school where he would be expected to answer questions, understand books and communicate with the teacher. He left our school transformed, and ready for the next step in his life. He went from being a boy who seemed surly and aggressive, and unable to be around other children without constant supervision, to a happy communicative child who enjoyed the company of other children and worked well in a group. Had he not attended our school, he could have graduated with a label of 'biter' or 'non-compliant' or 'aggressive' or 'difficult to handle.' But instead, he left us happy, outgoing, his own true kind and loving nature showing on his face.

Analysis of what worked for Francois:

We reflected on how just one year had helped Francois and his family a great deal. Once again, communication between parent and teacher to create a team had worked in the child's favor. Through that communication we came to understand the connection between his behavior and the family dynamics – the fact that Francois' sister was allowed to be in charge of him made him feel helpless and angry. Both school and family focusing on him in a loving and 'scientific' way made us all accountable to Francois. Acceptance was key here, as it is in all our interventions. We refused to react in an angry or punitive way to Francois' aggression. We accepted that behavior is a result of emotions, and we recognized here that the child's biting was an indication of his feeling of helplessness, due in part to his family situation, and also to the inability to communicate in English. Our acceptance of him made him feel safe, we did not yell or reprimand, we reacted with patience and understanding.

We knew that he needed safety first – by defending him in front of the other children we demonstrated that we were his protectors. And finally we knew that he needed vocabulary as a tool to protect himself. When we were no longer with him, he was going to need the words and phrases to take care of himself in any group situation he may encounter. By supplying him with phrases to express his needs and assert his boundaries, we felt it was like packing him a suitcase full of supplies that would carry him through on his journey to the next part of his school life.

Molly and her Brother

Molly and her brother joined us for our summer program. Daniel was the older brother and he was already 4 and a half so he would not be continuing with us for our fall semester, but Molly would be with us in our Threes class. Immediately we noticed that Daniel had some difficulties. He was very distressed on separation, and his parents were very anxious about him. They would stay in the classroom for extended periods of time and he would cling to his father's leg and refuse to let him leave, then he would cry after his father left. It took him a long time to adapt to the program, but when he did he seemed happy.

Molly, however, adapted quickly – right from the start – even though her older brother was crying, she played quietly and did not show any distress. She was the 'easy' one, as her mother said repeatedly in front of her. The summer program was 6 weeks long, and Daniel gradually became more comfortable, but we could see that, because he was shy, he got the lion's share of attention from both parents while Molly was counted on to be 'just fine.' He got hugs and promises of treats at the end of the day, while she got a quick wave and a goodbye. Molly kept to herself during the day, played with dolls or blocks, said very little and had a tightly closed mouth and a serious expression. She participated, but was quiet, and we all felt she had a lot to say but didn't say it.

When September rolled around, things were different. Now there was no Daniel, he was in another school, and Molly came to school accompanied by either her mother or her father. Molly entered the class just as she had in the summer, with a calm, resolute expression. She handled things well at first – a quick goodbye from her mom and she sat down with blocks and played quietly. That was just the first day, and it was a half-day. The second day was a full day. And that's when everything changed. She said goodbye to her mother. But soon as her mother left, Molly stood with her back to the wall while the other children became engaged with toys, and she scowled at anyone who looked at her.

When the teacher came over to ask if she was ready to hang up her backpack, she showed a snarling face, turned her head away, pulled her shoulders up, and in body language made it very clear that she was not going to move or talk to anyone. Now we saw a different side of Molly, and we knew she was about to show us her real feelings. She had been compliant and 'easygoing' before, but not any longer. We were happy about that, as we know how exhausting it must be for a child to keep feelings inside. And we knew that she must be feeling strange to be all alone, without her brother or her parents, in a new school. Though some of the children were people she'd known from the summer, there were quite a few new people she did not know.

The problem for Molly, we felt, was that her way of showing feelings was to isolate herself and not allow anyone to talk to her or help her. But it seemed the best thing to do at this point was to wait, we did not want to put any pressure on her, to rush her into conforming her behavior to our expectations, or to distract her from her feelings. The teachers let her stand against the wall for a while. Once or twice they would ask her a question, in case she was feeling like talking, but she would snarl. It was not a word really, just a growl, a warning that said: "Keep away. I am not going to cooperate with you." In a way we were glad to see that she was not being the 'easy' one any more. We were happy that we were one step closer to knowing who Molly was and how she felt. But this was a hard defense she was putting up.

That's when I decided that she needed an ally. When I entered the room and saw her standing against the wall she began to snarl as soon as she saw me looking at her. I felt at this point that she was alone and scared, and needed someone to recognize that, and to reach out to her – but not in a direct way, because she would reject any offer of help. I made up my mind to mirror what I thought she was feeling. So I said:

"I hope no one is looking at this girl. She doesn't like it!" I turned to Molly and said: "Is someone looking at you? How dare they! Is it him?" I pointed at the Head Teacher, Frank. "Is he bothering you? Is he looking at you?" Her eyes grew wide. She couldn't believe her luck, someone was speaking for her, expressing her inner feelings. She nodded tentatively. I snapped at the teacher, who understood what I was trying to do.

"She doesn't want anyone looking at her. Do you hear me?" The teacher played along with me.

"OK I'll go over here," he said, pretending to cover his eyes. "I won't look at her."

"Yes you do that! You go over there and don't bother her." I looked back at her. "I won't let anyone look at you!" I said. "You come to me if they do!" Then I turned to the teacher again. "You hear me? You leave her alone!" I could see that there was a tiny softening in Molly's face, a faint smile she couldn't control. She felt powerful. The teacher had to respect her feelings and not look at her. She was in charge.

Seeing Molly demonstrate resistance, I understood that she wanted to show her displeasure…she missed her father who had dropped her off earlier, and the teacher was a poor substitute for him. She also felt small and helpless and alone, and like an animal, she stood with her back to the wall, on guard. But she didn't feel able to express any of her feelings. Mirroring her feelings for her was a way of helping her to know she had an ally, someone who knew she had feelings she could not express. She would then not feel so alone. The rest of that day went a little better, she did sit down and participate with the class, but kept silent and did not contribute a word.

The next day, things got real! Once all the parents had left I went into the classroom to see how Molly was doing. When I opened the door it was obvious that there was something very dramatic going on. Molly was not quiet any longer, she was stamping her foot and slapping herself on the thigh, her face was red and she was saying "NO! NO! NO!" over again. Apparently she was not being asked to do anything, she was just protesting being left in school. It was another stage in her reaction to separation. She wasn't frozen any more, she was angry.

The Head Teacher stepped in to help, he knew that mirroring was a good technique to use with her, it had worked the day before. "This girl is angry!" he said, stamping his foot and grunting: "I know just how she feels!" She was not stamping now, she was just watching, but she was frowning and looked like she was ready to cry. She wasn't softening her stance, she was ready to stamp again if needed. Then Frank took a cardboard box that was lying around for art projects and he said:

"Molly is angry!" and he stomped on the box. Molly stared. She was completely silent. Frank trampled the box until it was flat. Molly's eyes were wide open, her brows were no longer darkening her expression. She was full of admiration. She enjoyed seeing other people show the emotion she was feeling inside. I spoke up again:

"Yes, we know what it's like to feel angry! I hope everybody around here knows that Molly is angry!" The other teachers smiled. I turned to Molly and said:

"Molly! You just remember, anyone bothers you, I will talk to them!" She nodded and gave a faint smile, I knew this was progress. "And just remember too, we're angry just like you! We won't stand for this!" And I walked away. There was no need to elaborate, to explain why we might be angry...Molly got the idea, it's ok to say you're angry, and it's ok to show it. We wanted to demonstrate acceptance *of her feelings, and to let her know that this is a safe space where someone can say they are angry, and no one tells them they can't say that. It was a kind of mirroring that we felt would let her get in touch with the anger she felt inside.*

The rest of that day turned out to be a good one for Molly. She came out of her corner, sat on the floor and started playing with blocks, right beside another girl. Pretty soon she had a doll and was walking around the class with the doll in a stroller, smiling to herself and talking to the doll. We knew we had crossed a bridge with her.

On the fourth day of school, when Molly's father left, she cried. A real, open cry. It was not anger, it was not fear or anxiety, it was a heartfelt expression of sadness at separating from a parent. When she cried she allowed the teacher to put her arm around her shoulder and tell her she knew how sad she was. It was probably a huge relief to her to be able to trust people enough to let herself show her deep feelings.

There are stages of grief, outlined by Elizabeth Kubler-Ross, and pre-school children do go through a process on separating that can in a way be described as grief. They experience a feeling of loss of a previous stage, and a realization that a new stage is happening. Molly had passed through stages of grief – she had moved from denial to anger and was now experiencing sadness, a final stage before her acceptance of change.

Molly was quiet for a long time, though she had passed through the stages of separation and seemed to be enjoying our class, she was still not fully participating. The teachers felt that they needed to somehow enable her to make friendships and be comfortable in the classroom. They noticed that she was very empathic. When a little girl fell in the playground and cried, Molly came over hesitantly, then bent down next to her and put her arm gently on her shoulder while the teacher put a band-aid on her knee. We realized she was very nurturing. She liked to play with babies and pretend to take care of them. And she liked to take care of other children.

We decided to take her and another child to the younger classroom at lunchtime so they could be helpers. Molly proved to be very good at helping to pour water for smaller children, to open up their lunch boxes, and even help to feed them if they needed it. She loved this role, and the little ones loved her. They would ask for her, and we would bring them up to visit her classroom so they could play there. Molly showed them the toys and played with them, she felt very responsible.

Molly made great progress after that. She started talking to us about things she liked. She was bubbly at story time, making observations and answering questions, and talking about the books she had at home. The teacher asked Molly's parents to send in something she liked so she could share it with others. She came in with a box of shells she'd found at the beach during the summer and she allowed everyone to pick them up and look at them. It didn't take her long to make a good friend, and soon she came in the door with a bounce in her step, and was a strong vocal member of the class.

By the end of the year, Molly was sad to leave. She did integrate well into her new school, and she came back to visit us frequently. She would say that she really missed our school. "This is my favorite school in the world," she told us. We were glad that she had proceeded through this initial separation from her family and learned that school can be a happy place. The socialization we do at an early stage is very important for children, and helps them adapt to the various schools they move on to.

In this case Molly was prevented from falling into a pattern that might not have helped her in a school with large classes and only one teacher – she may have ended up being withdrawn and isolated instead of becoming the kind, sociable, nurturing girl she was. She could have become depressed, withholding her anger and fear and putting a brave face on everything. In our school she first had to learn to get in touch with her anger and sadness and work through those negative feelings before she could feel happy.

Analysis of what worked for Molly:

Molly was angry at the world because she didn't want to be dropped at school, and she couldn't express that anger, so she kept herself very withdrawn and silent. This set up a wall which impeded Molly from joining in, and prevented her from finding happiness and friendship. We felt she needed to be allowed to show her anger instead of being distracted or told to cheer up. A child, or adult, needs to first be able to acknowledge what they are feeling before they can move on from that feeling.

Mirroring is a technique whereby an empathic adult can demonstrate what a child is feeling inside. The child instinctively relates to the adult's mirroring behavior, and knows on a deep level that the adult is feeling the child's feelings, and showing them to the world. By mirroring Molly's feelings, we helped her to feel that she was understood, accepted, and supported.

Creating an accepting space is very important for a child such as Molly, who needs to know she can feel safe to show whatever feelings she is having. When we demonstrated anger by stepping on a box, we were trying to show Molly that anger is acceptable and normal in our classroom. This allowed her to feel safe to show her negative emotions in the classroom. Once she was able to do this, she was able to move on to the next stage, and this led the way to her releasing her sadness.

When the teacher let Molly know that an adult was on her side and would support her if anyone bothered her, this gave her a sense of empowerment. Then communication with parents became important. We asked parents to share something from home in order to make a bridge between family and school. And finally we needed to help Molly to develop her own nurturing nature by bringing her to visit the younger children and allowing her to make meaningful relationships as well as feel important and needed.

Chapter 11

LIFETIME EFFECTS OF EMOTIONAL EDUCATION

The lifetime effects of an emotional education are many. A child is born with deep feelings, and these feelings are with us our whole lives long. From the first cry of rage that food is not arriving fast enough, to the teenage fear of social exclusion, to the pang of sadness at losing a parent, our feelings follow us wherever we go. We may express them in relationships, in safe spaces, in our families. But in general, we tend to keep them out of the way, under control, and strictly uninvited into the business arena. This has been the accepted way of dealing with our emotions when it comes to our work.

However, new studies are pointing to the fact that the best students, and the best workers, are those of us who are able to be in touch with our emotions and express them in healthy ways in social situations. Being socially adept helps us to be better students and workers. In fact there are new terms now in common use: Emotional Intelligence and EQ, which refer to a form of intelligence essential to success in work and life. These terms refer to a set of abilities in regard to managing emotions.

These abilities include:

Self awareness

This means the ability to be aware of what we are feeling and why. Knowing what you feel is the first step to being able to control your response. According to an article in Forbes Magazine, a study examined 72 executives at public and private companies with revenues from $50 million to $5 billion. This study found that:

> *Interestingly, a high self-awareness score was the strongest predictor of overall success. This is not altogether surprising as executives who are aware of their weaknesses are often better able to hire subordinates who perform well in categories in which the leader lacks acumen. These leaders are also more able to entertain the idea that someone on their team may have an idea that is even better than their own.*[20]

Self regulation

This means the ability to modify or adapt our behavior based on conscious choices rather than knee-jerk reactions. It is very important for children to learn this skill as it enhances performance and leads to greater success in school. A Duke University analysis of over 150 studies of self-regulation and school performance found that:

> *Taken together, the processes, domains, and underlying skills of self-regulation were significantly correlated with academic performance during the pivotal transition to formal schooling and the academic stages that follow it.*[21]

Social awareness

This means the ability to assess other people. It is a very complex skill and it involves observing the expressions and actions of others and understanding the motivations behind people's behavior. An article on the American Psychological Association's website concludes that SEL programs which foster social awareness, can also foster academic success:

An interesting synergy results when these programs are offered, Greenberg adds. When children are taught these skills, they learn how to foster their own well-being and become more resilient. That, in turn, builds a more positive classroom climate that better engages children in learning. And as they become more absorbed in learning, children are more likely to do better in school.[22]

Social competence

This means the ability to make friends, give and take, talk and listen, make others feel comfortable, be assertive but not aggressive, and so on, in order to feel that we are equal and important members of a group. Studies show that social competence in childhood is a good indicator of career success, as this Duke University study indicates:

Is it possible to predict a child's future based on her social competencies and behavior in kindergarten? A new study that followed 800 U.S. children from kindergarten through their mid-20s suggests it is. The study...found that kids who showed specific social competency traits in kindergarten were four times more likely to graduate college and have a full-time job by age 25. The study authors...note that the kindergarteners who demonstrated social competency traits such as being helpful, sharing with others, resolving problems with their peers and listening to others maintained these qualities through high school, college and beyond.[23]

Moral behavior

Children who grow up in an environment of emotional respect become autonomous, and make moral decisions of their own free will, rather than from strict adherence to authority. Healthy communities are built on moral behavior by people who respect other people's rights. According to renowned educational theorist Jean Piaget:

The cooperative teacher considers the child's point of view and encourages the child to consider others' points of view. The motive for co-operation begins in feelings of mutual affection

*and mutual trust which become elaborated into feelings of
sympathy and consciousness of the intentions of self
and others.*[24]

Self-Confidence

I have found that children who show their feelings tend to be
popular, they seem to play an important role in a group, perhaps
expressing feelings others cannot. Being able to express your
feelings in a constructive way, and having other people accept your
feelings, gives a child a sense of confidence and belonging
in the group.

> *Children who freely express all their feelings, excitement,
> sadness, anger, disappointment, tend to be popular with other
> children. It seems children trust others who are open and
> expressive. In our society actors, performers, film makers, are
> often held in high regard. In ancient Egypt, singers were
> considered almost as important as royalty. In ancient Ireland,
> poets lived in the company of kings. There is a good reason for
> all of this. These kinds of people are valued highly because they
> play a vital role in society.*[25]

No one is born with these abilities!! None of us at age six months can
understand what we are feeling, or regulate our feelings. At that age, we
can't properly tell, nor do we care, what others feel. And we certainly
don't know how to make friends and be part of a group, much less
keep others in mind. All these abilities are learned – or not learned,
which causes pretty much all the problems in our world. Emotional
competence can be learned, and we can never start too early to teach
children these valuable skills. At each age, we can focus on creating
developmentally appropriate ways of strengthening a child's
emotional intelligence.

So how does emotional intelligence help in a work situation? Success is
very highly correlated with emotional competence. There are many
indicators of how being in charge of our own feelings can help in work.
Having emotional competence, understanding others and managing
our own feelings, can make a huge difference in the success of any
child at school, or any adult at work. Take the quiz to see how well
you are doing.

Appendix

QUIZ:
ARE YOU EMOTIONALLY INTELLIGENT?

Take this quiz, and when you are done, score your answers at the end.

Ask yourself if you are more inclined towards A or B:

- A. *I am able to take criticism, process it and change and grow*
- B. *I am defensive when criticized*

- A. *I am able to face my mistakes and learn from them*
- B. *I blame others when things go wrong*

- A. *I spend time looking at the reasons why errors occur*
- B. *I cover up mistakes in a way that causes them to recur in the future*

- A. *I stay calm under pressure*
- B. *I panic and lose self control when things go wrong*

- A. *When I fail I decide to try again*
- B. *I give up because I can't bear to keep failing*

A. When I feel anxious about an exam or presentation I
find strategies to manage my jitters
B. I let anxiety get the better of me, avoid challenges,
or perform badly because I'm overwhelmed with fear

A. When someone confronts me with my error, I am able to
laugh at myself
B. I tend to get upset when my dignity is offended, and I try to
make sure that no one confronts me again

A. When someone is disappointed with me, I am able to accept
that their disappointment is an unfortunate outcome for them that
is not my problem
B. I go out of my way to make sure other people are not
upset by my decisions

A. I tend to ask other people at meetings what they think, and
I listen to their ideas and input
B. I make it clear to everyone that things are done my way

A. I am able to tell my boss that I think I deserve a raise
B. I feel resentful that no one appreciates me, even though
I don't ask for what I need

A. I am able to tell my colleague that I disagree with him
B. I tend to say nothing and go behind his back, telling other
people that he thinks he is always right

A. I can tell someone that I don't feel comfortable laughing at a
person who is different
B. I tend to go along with what the majority says because I want to
belong to the group

A. I can tell a colleague if I need space and quiet to work
B. I tend to put up with constant interruptions because I feel I
don't want to upset people

A. I generally focus on the task at hand and pay attention to
what is going on
B. I get frequently distracted by the feelings running around
in my head

A. *I usually know it when I'm feeling angry about something and I share my angry feelings with a supportive friend*
B. *I tend to lash out at people at work or school without knowing what's bothering me*

A. *I tend to notice when someone else is feeling sad or unusually quiet*
B. *I often talk to fill the silence, even if I get no response*

A. *I trust my own impressions and judgments*
B. *I tend to make decisions and regret that I didn't listen to my first instincts*

A. *I find satisfaction in doing work that I really love*
B. *I am in a career that others thought would be good for me, and I can't change because I am afraid to disappoint them*

A. *I enjoy being friendly and welcoming to clients*
B. *I tend to be angry at having to interact with demanding people*

A. *I run my business in a way that helps my employees fulfill themselves and take on more responsibilities*
B. *I like to keep employees under my watchful eye to make sure nothing goes wrong*

A. *I make time to listen to employees' complaints and suggestions*
B. *I feel annoyed that people can't just do their job and leave their emotions at home*

A. *I would go to work even though I don't feel great, because people really need me*
B. *I would stay home when I'm feeling a bit tired because 'they' don't appreciate me anyway*

A. *I make lists of my goals and try to stay on track*
B. *I just tackle problems one by one as they come along*

A. *I try to stay at jobs and work my way up to a better position*
B. *I tend to move from one job to the next when things don't work out*

EMOTIONAL EDUCATION

A. *I would try looking around to find a more fulfilling job than the one I am in*
B. *I have been staying in the same job year after year because I am afraid to make a change*

A. *I make a schedule for when and how I work or study, based on what I know about myself and my work or study habits*
B. *I often beat myself up because I don't work or study the same way other people do*

A. *I know my own weaknesses – I would turn down a position that I feel is just not right for me*
B. *I take on stressful projects because other people tell me they would be good for my career*

A. *I join organizations that can make a change in my community*
B. *I often complain that things are not the way they should be*

A. *I am willing to change and do things a new way*
B. *I tend to stick to things that have worked well so far*

A. *I am willing to stick to my principles and do things the way I believe is right*
B. *I change my approach based on what I think people want me to do*

Scoring: Give yourself one point for every A answer, zero for B answers.

SCORE: 20-30 You are emotionally adept and chances are you're a big success

SCORE: 10-20 Brush-up required – you need to get more in touch with your feelings

SCORE: 1-10 You need Emotional Education

NOTES

1 seop.illc.uva.nl/entries/emotion/Revised Jan 21, 2013

2 Hume, John (1739) *Treatise* Book 2.3.3, (page 415)

3 Hume, John (1739) *Treatise* Book 2.1.4.3, (page 283)

4 Borba, Michele A. (2016) *Unselfie* Simon & Schuster, NY (page 24)

5 Parens, Henri (1993), *Aggression in Our Children, Coping with it Constructively,* Jason Aronson, NJ (page 2)

6 Hayward, Karen, et al (2009) *Educating for Gross National Happiness in Bhutan* Draft Sourcebook Volume 3 part 1. Compiled by GPI Atlantic

7 Goleman, Daniel (2006) *Emotional Intelligence: Why It Can Matter More Than IQ* Random House, NY (page 284)

8 Gabrieli, Ansel, et al Dec (2015) *Ready to be Counted: The Research Case for Education Policy Action on Non-Cognitive Skills* Transforming Education V.01 (page 10)

[9] Bettelheim, Bruno, and Karen Zelan (1982) *On Learning to Read: The Child's Fascination with Meaning,* Knopf, NY

[10] Quantz, Richard A. (2003) *The Puzzlemasters: Performing the Mundane, Searching for Intellect, and Living in the Belly of the Corporation.* The Review of Education, Pedagogy, and Cultural Studies V. 25 95-137 (page 113).

[11] Henderlong-Corpus, C. et al (2006) *The Effects of Social-Comparison versus Mastery Praise on Children's Intrinsic Motivation.* Motivation and Emotion 30:335-345 (page 344)

[12] http://www.newsweek.com/why-has-teacher-morale-plummeted-321447

[13] Neill, A. S. *Summerhill* (1960) *A Radical Approach to Child Rearing.* Hart Publishing, NY

[14] Broadbent, Donald (1982) *Task combination and selective intake of information.* Acta Psychol (Amst). Jul;50(3) (pp: 253-90) *The Domain of Supervisory Processes and Temporal Organization of Behaviour.* Shallice, et al, also *PhilosophicalTransactions: Biological Sciences,* The Royal Society, Vol.351, No.1346

[15] Fox, Mem (2003) *Harriet, You'll Drive Me Wild!* Harcourt Books

[16] http://www.parentguidenews.com/Articles/TheBeautyOfTears

[17] Bettelheim, Bruno (1972) *The Empty Fortress: Infantile Autism and the Birth of the Self.* Macmillan Publishing, NY (page 3)

[18] Stone, Jon and Smollin, Michael (2003) *The Monster at the End of this Book.* Random House Golden Books, NY

[19] *Aristotle Poetics, Book 6.2*

[20] http://www.forbes.com/sites/victorlipman/2013/11/18/all-successful leaders-need-this-quality-self-awareness/#6cbaf1d657b4

21 http://dukespace.lib.duke.edu/dspace/bitstream/handle/10161/7265/Dent_duke_0066D_11985.pdf?sequence=1

22 http://www.apa.org/monitor/2010/04/classrooms.aspx

23 https://www.interviewedge.com/articles/social-competencies.htm

24 http://www.uni.edu/coe/regentsctr/Publications/Piagets%20Social%20Theory.pdf

25 Johnson, Eileen (2014) *The Children's Bill of Emotional Rights,* Jason Aronson, MD (page 255)

INDEX

Made in the USA
Middletown, DE
22 March 2017